FRAGMENTS IN THE RUINS

About Policy Network

Policy Network is the international ideas exchange for progressives. More than just a thinktank, its network spans national borders across Europe and the wider world with the aim of promoting the best progressive thinking on the major social and economic challenges of the 21st century.

What makes Policy Network unique is our ability to connect policymakers and policy implementers. We combine rigorous analysis of the biggest questions facing modern societies with creative thinking on how to turn those fresh solutions into dynamic political narratives that can deliver electoral success for progressive parties.

A platform for research and ideas

- Promoting expert ideas and political analysis on the key economic, social and political challenges of our age.
- Disseminating research excellence and relevant knowledge to a wider public audience through interactive policy networks, including interdisciplinary and scholarly collaboration.
- Engaging and informing the public debate about the future of European and global progressive politics.
- Building international policy communities comprising individuals and affiliate institutions.
- Providing meeting platforms where the politically active, and potential leaders of the future, can engage with each other across national borders, with the best thinkers who are sympathetic to their broad aims.
- Engaging in external collaboration with partners including higher education institutions, the private sector, thinktanks, charities, community organisations, and trade unions
- Delivering an innovative events programme combining in-house seminars with large-scale public conferences designed to influence and contribute to key public debates.

www.policynetwork.org @policynetwork

FRAGMENTS IN THE RUINS

The Renewal of Social Democracy

David Coats

}{
policy network

ROWMAN & LITTLEFIELD
INTERNATIONAL

London • New York

Published by Rowman & Littlefield International Ltd.
Unit A, Whitacre Mews, 26-34 Stannary Street, London SE11 4AB
www.rowmaninternational.com

Rowman & Littlefield International Ltd. is an affiliate of Rowman & Littlefield
4501 Forbes Boulevard, Suite 200, Lanham, Maryland 20706, USA
With additional offices in Boulder, New York, Toronto (Canada), and Plymouth (UK)
www.rowman.com

British Library Cataloguing in Publication Data
A catalogue record for this book is available from the British Library

ISBN: PB 978-1-78660-833-8
ISBN: eBook 978-1-78660-834-5

Library of Congress Cataloging-in-Publication Data

Library of Congress Control Number: 2018952216

"These fragments I have shored against my ruins"
T. S. Eliot, The Waste Land

CONTENTS

ABOUT THE AUTHOR

David Coats is the director of WorkMatters Consulting. He has been a research fellow at the Smith Institute since 2010 and in 2014 he was appointed as a visiting professor at the Centre for Sustainable Work and Employment Futures, University of Leicester.

From 2004–2010 he was associate director – policy at The Work Foundation. From 1999–2004 he was head of the Trades Union Congress' economic and social affairs department, having first joined the TUC in 1989 as an employment law specialist.

He has been a member of the Labour party for 36 years.

FOREWORD

Despite the title, this volume is not intended to be an obituary for social democracy. It is inspired by the belief that the values that have sustained British and European progressives for the last century or more are of continuing relevance in what can only be described as the most challenging political environment of the last seventy years. Intellectual confidence is a precursor of political confidence and the mainstream centre left requires a profound intellectual renewal. We will not, in Anthony Crosland's words, win a battle of ideas by looking for oracular guidance from sacred texts. The task is to rethink social democracy's central purpose in relation to the world as we find it today.

I make no apology for the fact that there are more questions than answers presented here. It is a historic weakness of the British left that over-commitment to particular programmatic prescriptions has stifled debate and created a culture where factional victory inside the Labour Party is viewed as a necessary condition for electoral success. My case, to the contrary, is that Labour is most successful when it is open, pluralist and tolerant, recognising the multiplicity of sources contributing to the progressive stream and bringing diverse opinions into alignment behind a programme that is both practical and radical. Whether I have achieved that objective is for readers to judge.

I would like to thank Patrick Diamond, Matthew Laza and Alex Porter at Policy Network for their support throughout the writing process and for their patience with an author who often gave the impression that brevity was a principle to be breached rather than observed. Roger Liddle offered valuable insights into Labour's approach to planning and regional policy in the 1960s and encouraged me to believe that the project was worth completing. All errors and infelicities are of course my own.

Finally, I owe a debt of gratitude to my partner, Joanne Segars, who kept me focused on the task in hand. Without her I would still be writing, revising and polishing. Thank you for helping me to get it done.

THE WORLD TURNED UPSIDE DOWN

A story about the past and the present

*The old is dying and the new cannot be born; in this interregnum
there arises a great diversity of morbid symptoms.*

Antonio Gramsci, *The Prison Notebooks* (1929–1936)

TWO SONGS

An early recorded use of the expression "the world turned upside
down" dates from the middle 1640s, during the English civil war,
when a popular ballad decried the prohibition of the usual Christmas
celebrations by a Puritan-dominated parliament – a historical example, perhaps, of a protest against 'political correctness gone mad'.
The phrase has achieved more recent currency through Billy Bragg's
version of Leon Rosselson's song in praise of the Diggers, the civil
war-era radical Christian sect, often seen as a proto-socialist movement: "this earth divided, we will make whole, so it can be a common treasury for all". Extreme times produce extreme responses.
On the one hand reaction, a hankering for the past, a lament for
something that has been lost; on the other, a utopian hope for a better world.

A similar dynamic is at work today, even though the times may be a little less extreme. The desire for historic certainties about the nation, order, rules and tradition all constitute a new common sense on the right, particularly in the US and the UK. On the left, a belief in the necessity of change, the imperative to root out injustice and the yearning for a new social order has spawned movements led by individuals, like Bernie Sanders and Jeremy Corbyn, previously beached on the margins of politics for more than 30 years.

Today the world is confronted by realities that would have been viewed as beyond credibility a decade ago. It would have seemed implausible that a candidate like Donald Trump could become president of the US. Hostile to open trade, belligerent and irresponsible in foreign policy, explicitly racist and sexist – all this would have consigned any 'normal' politician to electoral oblivion.

Most politicians, commentators and engaged citizens had taken the UK's membership of the EU as a fact of life for more than 40 years. Yet a deep-rooted political and economic partnership is now about to end with no suggestion that the UK will be able to negotiate a superior arrangement in the future. When measured against 'normal' political assumptions, the 2016 referendum result can only be viewed as a catastrophic act of self-harm. Why would citizens of the UK vote to make the country poorer, less influential on the global stage and a supplicant at the feet of more powerful nations? The future post-Brexit looks less than inviting for those with a progressive cast of mind. A brave new world beckons of lopsided trade agreements requiring the import of chlorine-washed chicken, hormone-treated beef and the opening up of the NHS as a business opportunity for US healthcare providers. The world has been turned upside down.

Nobody foresaw the return of the far right to the German Bundestag or the presence of parties, often with explicitly fascist roots, in parliaments across the Nordic countries. No reputable commentator would have predicted a crisis of social democracy in continental Europe, with well-established parties struggling to survive, often experiencing wipeouts at the polls.

In a narrower, national context, any suggestion that the British Labour party, led by Jeremy Corbyn, could win 40% of the vote and deprive a Conservative government of its majority would have been treated as a far-fetched and not especially amusing joke. It was an established fact that progressive parties could only make progress if they fought on the centre-ground. Features of political life previously considered to be immutable have apparently transformed themselves into illusions or deceptions. The world has been turned upside down.

THE GLOBAL FINANCIAL CRISIS AS AN EXPLANATION?

A conventional account of recent events would locate the beginnings of this *bouleversement* in the global financial crisis of 2007–2009. It is certainly true that the crisis called into question most of the assumptions that had provided the rationale for economic policymaking in the UK and the US since the end of the 1970s. The belief in unconstrained free markets, small states, low taxes, limited regulation and the privatisation of public assets were all subjected to forensic interrogation, not least by some who had been the most enthusiastic proponents of the pre-crisis status quo.[1]

At the heart of the model was the view that economic actors (in this case global investment banks) were entirely rational and had an unchallengeable capacity to make sensible judgements about their own best interests. That this belief, more accurately described as faith, proved to be wholly false was recognised by Alan Greenspan, at that time the chairman of the Federal Reserve, in his oral evidence to the US Congress in 2008:

> *I made a mistake in presuming that the self-interest of organisations, specifically banks and others, were such that they were best capable of protecting their own shareholders and their equity in the firms. . . . This modern risk-management paradigm held sway for decades . . . the whole intellectual edifice collapsed in the summer of last year.*

This is as close to intellectual regicide as one might imagine. Imperial and imperious finance had been dethroned. No civil war, certainly, but by the standards of conventional, pre-crisis economics the world *had* been turned upside down.

This story about the crisis and its aftermath offers some insight into the UK's predicament, but it cannot really explain the deeper roots of the malaise. Austerity and the failure of the banking system alone cannot account for Brexit, the rising level of hostility to 'foreigners' (not a uniquely British phenomenon) or the rise of the far right across Europe and in the US. Nor can austerity and the behaviour of the banks completely explain increasing scepticism about 'globalisation', the anxiety that the economy is 'rigged' against the interests of ordinary people or the popular view that the prosperity most developed countries have taken for granted will simply not be available for future generations. To understand these phenomena we need to carry out a broader historical assessment. We need to talk about capitalism, socialism and democracy.

CAPITALISM: INCONVENIENT TRUTHS FOR RIGHT AND LEFT

For more than 50 years parties of the centre left, especially the mainstream of the British Labour party, have found it hard to offer a comprehensive, critical assessment of capitalism, often avoiding the word completely and preferring expressions like the mixed economy, the market economy or less than lapidary formulations like Tony Blair's "economic dynamism and social justice". There was a troubling feeling that using language with the slightest whiff of Marxism might do serious damage to the left's electoral prospects.[2]

The ambiguity meant that politicians on the centre left were not as clear as they might have been in explaining their intentions to the electorate, nor were they explicit about the undeniable benefits *and* disadvantages of capitalism. Moreover, in the UK (and perhaps in other parts of Europe too) there was a disjunction between the realities of progressive government in action and the expectations of party members, many of whom still hankered after social transformation. By failing to develop a compelling intellectual framework for progressive politics, most politicians on the mainstream centre left had very little persuasive to say in the wake of the crisis. There was an ideological vacuum that would, in due course, be filled by a nostalgic, old left politics, which only looked new, especially to young people, because it had been locked in cryogenic suspension for the preceding 30 years.

To make progress with our discussion we need to define our terms. Just what do we mean when we talk about capitalism? Most dictionary definitions are a little bloodless, but they do capture the essentials of the system. Private ownership, competition, profit and market prices are the principal features of the system. But if we really want to understand what has happened in the economy since (say) 1750 a number of additional ingredients are required in the definitional mix.

First, the emergence of capitalism was associated with a high degree of urbanisation, a move from rural, agricultural or craft employment to work in a factory system.

Second, this process was historically associated with a decline in the quality of living and working conditions for the new urban working class, a phenomenon documented in the 19th century by social investigators like Friedrich Engels (*The Condition of the Working Class in England,* 1845), Henry Mayhew (*Labour and the London Poor,* 1851) and Charles Booth (*Life and Labour of the People,* 1889). Certainly, progress had been made on public health by the end of the nineteenth century – with clean water in most British cities, a decent sewerage system and a decline in infectious diseases – but in 1889 more than a third of Londoners were living in "abject poverty" on Booth's definition. The first pamphlet published by the Fabian Society in 1884 was entitled *Why Are the Many Poor?* There was a consensus on the left that capitalism was not providing significant benefits for the majority of citizens. Only the institution of a completely new social order could guarantee decent lives for all.

Third, despite the realities of widespread poverty in nineteenth-century Britain, the period since 1750 has witnessed a dramatic increase in the growth of productivity across the world and a transformation of both incomes and living standards for the majority of the population. This is the inconvenient truth about capitalism to which the left must respond.

Fourth, alongside the potential for productivity growth, capitalism creates a higher degree of uncertainty in the lives of people who have no source of support but income from work. In part, this can be explained by fluctuations in unemployment determined by the operation of the business cycle. More important, however, is the fifth feature of a capitalist economy: the interaction of capital, technology and competition. This is manifested in what the Austrian economist Joseph Schumpeter described as "creative destruction" (Schumpeter 1943). In a technological battle for survival those companies with newer, more attractive products and services or more efficient processes will defeat those that fail to adapt. Creative destruction is an important notion because it explains how whole industries can die and new industries take their place. It is competition, capital and technology in combination that lead to the production of new goods and services.

It is essential to understand the extent to which people were exposed to new dangers by capitalism. In rural, agricultural societies the risks to individuals and their families were very different. Work was dictated by the rhythms of the seasons; harvests could fail, there might be natural disasters, wars conducted at the discretion of an aristocratic elite or the devastation wrought by infectious diseases. Nonetheless, the pace of change was slow. Life for the majority of the rural population altered very little from one century to another. A farmer from the first dynasty period in ancient Egypt (approximately 5,000 years ago) would, absent the difficulties of language and differences in religious ritual, have had little trouble in understanding the life of a peasant in eighteenth-century Europe. Both would be baffled, if not terrified, by the world today.[3]

Arguably, it is the phenomenon of creative destruction, rather than the business cycle, that has posed more difficulties for policymakers and more practical challenges for citizens. It is creative destruction that accounts for the real differences in productivity between different regions in the UK, for the fact that some localities have yet to recover from the loss of their traditional sources of employment in the 1980s and for the inconvenient truth that capitalism, left to itself, creates radical insecurity for far too many people. As Schumpeter observed, this is the essential dynamic of the system.[4] A failure to recognise that reality and take appropriate action to protect those most at risk lies at the root of many of the problems confronting developed western countries today. Markets are brutal in their operation, even though they remain the best system yet devised for the efficient distribution of many (but by no means all) goods and services. This is the inconvenient truth about capitalism to which the left must respond.

That the many in the developed world are *not* now poor would have surprised those social investigators who documented the failures of capitalism in the nineteenth century. Certainly, the stubborn residue of poverty might still trouble them, but nobody in Manchester now lives in the conditions described by Engels.[5] Nobody dies of cholera. Nobody starves. Of course, it would be wrong to attribute undeniable social progress to capitalism alone. Over the course of the past century and a half the feral beast of the early nineteenth century has been tamed, domesticated and civilised. Organised groups, most notably the labour movement, made what were initially seen as unreasonable demands – universal suffrage, free education, healthcare free at the point of need, support for the unemployed, decent housing for all – which, once met and combined with capital, markets and technology, produced the increases in prosperity that transformed the lives of the citizens of the developed world. Nonetheless, it took almost a century of struggle to create the institutions of the welfare state that were, until relatively recently, taken for granted throughout the rich west. Both the creation of capitalism and its evolution into a system that delivered unprecedented improvements in living standards required deliberate and decisive political action.

CIVILISING CAPITALISM: THE SYMBIOSIS OF PUBLIC AND PRIVATE

What this brief account also suggests is that it makes little sense to talk about 'capitalism' as a single, undifferentiated phenomenon. The economy described in Adam Smith's *The Wealth of Nations* (1775) shares few institutional features with the arrangements that prevail today. Despite the common elements of markets, competition and private ownership, Smith's economy was essentially national, international trade was on a relatively small scale, industrial production was in its infancy, most people still worked on the land, there was no developed welfare state, giant corporations with political interests of their own had yet to be born and the banking system was, by modern standards, relatively simple to understand.

Moreover, the development of capitalism since the industrial revolution has not followed a linear path. It has been a process characterised by mutation, adaptation, false starts, catastrophic mistakes (the Great Depression and the global financial crisis) and radical remedies, all of which have had the effect of preserving the central elements of the system adumbrated in the dictionary definition.

Capitalism today is not, therefore, the capitalism described by Smith. In the absence of the public provision of health and education it is unlikely that employers would have access to healthy and well-educated workers. Without investment in public infrastructure the UK would lack a decent road network, clean water and a secure supply of energy (Lindert 2004). Whether through regulatory activity or direct provision, the state plays an indispensable role in facilitating the operation of markets. Indeed, there is a strong case for saying that, far from being expressions of a spontaneous order, markets are and have always been dependent on the action of public authority.

Inherent in the notion of a market order is the belief that sometimes people will break the rules and that these rules need to be enforced. That is why the law of contract exists, why the criminal law prohibits fraud and why, if one person's use of their property causes damage to another, civil remedies are available to compensate for loss.

In general, however, most transactions in markets rarely attract the direct attention of the law. Contracts are concluded and completed successfully principally because each party trusts the other to discharge their side of the bargain. The state establishes the framework of rules that both prohibits bad behaviour and creates the trust on which the market depends.

The state also intervenes to protect people against abuses of power in markets. Economists very often express this idea through the notion of 'information asymmetries' where, for example, a seller of goods and services (say a second-hand car or a pension policy) knows a good deal more than the customer about what precisely is on offer (Akerlof 1970). In this context, the superior knowledge of one party to the transaction confers power and creates ample opportunities for unscrupulous behaviour.

Consumer protection legislation, of which the rules on consumer credit are a good example, is designed to correct this information asymmetry. If the rules are either too weak or completely absent then the public will be exploited – witness, for example, the mis-selling of personal pensions, endowment mortgages and payment protection insurance. The same might be said of labour market regulation, where statutory minimum wage-setting machinery and the framework of employment rights compensate for unequal bargaining power. And the argument applies with even greater force to the operation of the financial system, as the global crisis has demonstrated with some brutality. If government fails to set the stage and fix the background conditions for the operation of markets then somebody, somewhere will be at a significant disadvantage.

THE POSTWAR SETTLEMENT 1945–1980

Most of the institutions of the welfare state that we take for granted today are the result of action taken by Clement Attlee's Labour government. Yet, while Attlee and his colleagues are celebrated in the UK for a unique achievement, parties of the centre right and left, across Europe and North America, were devising broadly similar institutions to reduce the insecurities to which citizens were exposed. In part, this was because of the Keynesian revolution in economics. Governments of all political hues accepted their responsibility to maintain full employment, or at least to avoid the mass unemployment that had done such damage in the 1930s. Policymakers believed, not without reason, that this end could be achieved by the judicious use of public spending to sustain the level of economic activity through what would otherwise have been a severe recession.

In the UK in the early 1950s, the argument between Labour and the Conservatives concerned the boundaries of the state and the private sector; how much more of the economy should be nationalised? There were also disputes about the end of rationing, levels of tax and spending and intense disagreements about foreign policy – of which the Suez crisis in 1956 is the most notable example. But Conservative governments in the UK were happy to operate within the social policy framework established between 1945–1951; the architecture of the NHS and social security were left largely intact.

In his report for the wartime coalition government published in 1942, William Beveridge identified five giant evils that stalked the capitalist land: want, disease, ignorance, squalor and idleness. These evils could not be dealt with simply by leaving markets to themselves. The outcomes for citizens were intolerable in a democratic society, proving Schumpeter's point that democratic electorates were unwilling to accept the disadvantages of unrestrained capitalism. What most citizens appeared to want was *security* and this is what Beveridge and the 1945–1951 Labour government offered. Security of income, security of employment, security that healthcare would be available when needed, wider access to education and a safe, warm, comfortable home. In large measure these expectations were met by the middle 1950s. The risks that had caused such misery in the 1930s had been successfully ameliorated. But what the postwar settlement did not and could not achieve was an end to creative destruction.

Whatever may have been done after 1945, however the boundaries between public and private sectors may have been redrawn, nothing had altered the fundamental Schumpeterian dynamic. Developed country economies remained essentially capitalist; most goods and services were distributed in markets, with prices the outcome of a competitive process. While the pursuit of full employment and the construction of the postwar welfare state were effective in preventing a recurrence of the conditions of the 1930s, the policy orientation seemed to assume a stable, linear path of development. Apparently, it was believed that so long as intelligent economic planning could match labour demand to supply, technological and entrepreneurial disruption were no threat to security. This proved to be a major weakness in the postwar model as policymakers struggled to cope when confronted with new sources of international competition or technological threats to well-established forms of industrial employment. In other words, a policy solution devised to meet the challenges of the 1930s became less and less effective in the 1960s and 1970s.

This is not to say that the post-1945 settlement was a failure, simply that it proved to be insufficient in dealing with the challenges thrown up by features of capitalism other than the business cycle. These problems became increasingly acute in the 1960s and 1970s and still perplex policymakers today in a global economy that is far more integrated and with a much higher volume of international trade.

Indeed, by the end of the 1970s, the postwar settlement was under attack in both the UK and the US. Margaret Thatcher and Ronald Reagan both saw an expansive state as part of the problem. Over-mighty trade unions were responsible for inflation. A generous system of support for the unemployed and households with low incomes sapped individual initiative and undermined personal responsibility. If business was set free from regulatory constraints and individuals were compelled to stand on their own two feet then the economy would flourish and everybody would be better off.

DID THATCHERISM DELIVER ITS PROMISE?

If we judge Thatcherism by its results then one is driven to the conclusion that the policy prescription failed to deliver the promised outcomes. Inflation was certainly tamed, but at the expense of high levels of unemployment through to the early 1990s. Mismanagement of the currency and a deflationary budget during a global recession had the effect of making much of British industry uncompetitive, leading to a rapid decline in the number of manufacturing jobs. Taxes for the most affluent were reduced and rewards for those at the top of the income distribution became increasingly disconnected from wage growth for the majority. Executive pay was on an upward spiral. Financial markets were deregulated, with the state adopting a 'light touch' from 1986 onwards – but deregulation led directly to multiple financial scandals and the banking crisis of 2007–2009, when Alan Greenspan's paradigm failed.

Increased inequality

Income inequality rose rapidly in the 1980s but has remained relatively stable since that time. Inequality fell in the wake of the crisis and now sits below the pre-crisis level, although the difference is small (Figure 1.1). Some Conservatives might argue that income inequality is a natural outcome of the operation of markets and therefore one ought not to worry too much about the gap between rich and poor. But as the Organisation for Economic Co-operation and Development has pointed out, excessive income inequality produces a range of unwelcome social outcomes, including poorer health and shorter life expectancy for those in the lower reaches of the income distribution (OECD 2011). Moreover, there is strong evidence to show that unequal societies experience lower rates of growth, leaving aside the potential risks to social cohesion and the legitimacy of economic and political institutions (Berg and Ostry 2010). Reducing inequality is not just good for social justice but good for the economy too. To date, however, successive British

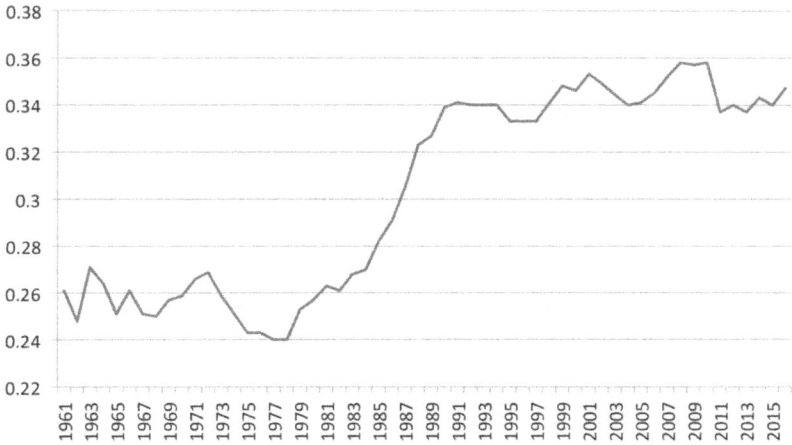

Figure 1.1   Income inequality in the UK, 1961–2016 (Gini coefficient). *Source:* Institute for Fiscal Studies.

governments have failed to reverse the big increases in inequality that took place in the 1980s.

Wage stagnation and the decoupling of wages from productivity

We observed earlier that capitalism's great achievement has been to secure high productivity growth, which has led to rising wages and living standards for the majority of the population. As a general proposition about the last two centuries this observation is accurate but since the early-middle 1990s something rather strange has happened in the UK. For all those on median incomes and below, wage growth has fallen behind the growth of productivity. In other words, all those workers in the bottom half of the income distribution are not receiving their fair share of the fruits of growth. The system is no longer working for them (Commission on Living Standards 2012, Pessoa and van Reenen 2012). The pay/productivity disconnection is not a universal phenomenon across all developed countries, which suggests that the cause must be something specific to the UK (Bailey et al. 2011).

The pay and productivity disconnection has been compounded by wage stagnation since the global financial crisis, and earnings growth has been at its weakest for more than a century, with a severe squeeze on living standards. The IFS forecasts that incomes for the bottom fifth of the population will fall over the next five years (Cribb et al. 2017). The UK is a low-pay economy with one in five workers earning less than two thirds of the median. This figure has remained the same for more than two decades, although the introduction of the national minimum wage has virtually eliminated 'extreme low pay', defined as earnings of less than half the median. Nonetheless, current policy seems to have exhausted its potential and further progress in reducing the reliance on low pay will require a more sophisticated set of policies – considered further in Chapter 3 and Chapter 4.

Regional imbalances

Prosperity in the UK is also very badly distributed across the regions. London and the greater south-east of England are amongst the most prosperous places in the world but beyond cities or towns with world-class universities the picture is much less attractive. The restructuring of the 1980s has left deep scars on the economy and on communities previously dependent on a single industry and its supply chain. The worst-affected regions and localities still experience unemployment at levels twice the national average and even where unemployment is low, wages are low too – Stoke-on-Trent and Mansfield are good examples of the second phenomenon.

NEW LABOUR IN POWER 1997–2010

Nothing done by Labour in power managed to rectify the damage caused by the industrial upheaval of the 1980s and 1990s. Regional policy was successful up to a point, regenerating the central districts of major cities in the north of England like Manchester, Leeds and Newcastle. But towns on the peripheries of these conurbations saw few benefits beyond the undoubted advantages conferred by new schools and hospitals. While the national minimum wage and tax credits improved the position of low-income families and Sure Start centres offered new routes to escape poverty, the fundamentals of the economic system bequeathed to New Labour by the Tories were left untouched. Beyond some increased investment in vocational training, little more was done to equip people with the confidence to ride the wave of creative destruction. Economic change was still leaving too many people feeling like casualties or victims rather than participants in an economy in which they had a meaningful stake.

It would be wrong to be too critical of the 1997–2010 Labour governments; much that was done was admirable but in retrospect looks more like tinkering than an effort to construct a new model out of the Thatcherite legacy. Labour markets (absent the national minimum wage) remained flexible; the governance of corporations was left to senior executives alone, acting under the tutelage of investors with very short-term horizons; there was no re-regulation of financial markets, no changes to the taxation of top incomes and no effort to restrain the excessive rewards available to the denizens of Britain's boardrooms. The government appeared to believe that it had limited room for manoeuvre. Any initiative that challenged the fundamentals of the post-1979 settlement was seen as a recipe for electoral catastrophe. And Labour, above all else, wanted to win and keep winning.

A great deal more could be said about the experience of Labour in government but the simplest way to characterise the UK's current position is that all governments, of whatever political hue, whether Conservative, coalition or Labour have accepted the institutional legacy of Thatcherism, either with alacrity, or hesitation, or distaste.

POPULISM, THE CRISIS AND CREATIVE DESTRUCTION

We can summarise our story so far as follows: capitalism is an efficient system for the distribution of most goods and services; it delivers rising incomes for the majority of the population. But capitalism destroys as well as creates, is subject to intermittent crises and injects a radical element of insecurity into the lives of most citizens. Governments in the postwar period constructed breakwaters and flood defences to prevent people being overwhelmed by the destructive effects of economic change. These policies were designed for an economy where most people at work were men, working full time, and often in industrial employment. Macroeconomic policy was designed to achieve and sustain full employment. A contributory social security system would provide income support when people did lose their jobs. The state would act to ensure that all citizens had access to major social goods like health, education and housing. Taxes raised from a growing economy would fund public expenditure and encourage further growth. In the postwar world, the state was operating a well-developed system of collective insurance against multiple risks.

All this was thrown into question in the 1970s as a consequence of turbulence in currency markets and rising oil prices, both of which created severe inflationary pressures. The history of the Conservative governments of the 1980s and 1990s is a careful dismantling of the institutional infrastructure that protected citizens against the damaging consequences of capitalism. The Blair and Brown governments did much to improve the position of households with low incomes, invested in public services but left much of the Thatcherite legacy intact. The social fractures that Labour inherited in 1997 had only been partially repaired 10 years later.

When the crisis came in 2007–2009 the sources of what manifested later as populist discontent were flowing into a growing stream. The casualties of Thatcherism, the large number of people who were already experiencing a squeeze on wages, those who had lost a sense of identity and self-respect in the upheaval of industrial restructuring were ready to respond to the populists' siren song. Immigrants and the EU became the *casus belli*, even if hostility to 'foreigners' and 'Europe' were merely unpleasant proxies for the manifestation of latent and genuine discontents.

This is a very British story – with echoes in the US, perhaps. But populism of the right (and left) is a problem for mainstream progressives across Europe. In the UK this manifests as support for Brexit and elsewhere in support for parties often located beyond the pale of the acceptable right. What else might be said to explain why Europe's stable political systems have been turned upside down?

VARIETIES OF CAPITALISM, GLOBALISATION AND IMMIGRATION

Globalisation in question

Much of economic disruption experienced before the global financial crisis is often attributed to 'globalisation'. This phenomenon, which essentially means an increasing volume of international trade, with intensifying competition, widespread integration of markets and supply chains and the free movement of capital is held responsible for a series of social ills. The decline of manufacturing is attributed to the rise of major new players on the global stage, principally China; income inequality is also supposedly a consequence of international trade because those with higher-level skills in developed countries are increasingly in demand, while those with lower-level skills are exposed to competition from low-wage workers across the world. Wage stagnation across the developed world is said to be another indication of the same phenomenon. Without globalisation, the financial crisis could have been contained in the US. It was precisely because financial institutions in Europe and North America had invested in dubious financial instruments produced largely on Wall Street that the contagion spread so rapidly across all the major economies.[6]

While the account of the financial crisis is correct, attributing all the other phenomena to globalisation is either an over-interpretation or a misreading of the situation. Developed countries have experienced significant disruption from the 1960s onwards, with employment in established industries declining or disappearing completely.[7] A shift in employment from manufacturing to services has been ubiquitous across the OECD, but this is a result of techno-logical change and productivity growth rather than a consequence of 'globalisation'.

Income inequality rose rapidly in the UK in the 1980s, principally because of domestic policy decisions. Labour market deregulation, the erosion of trade union power, the weakening of the welfare state and reductions in taxation for the most affluent were not mandated by changes in the global economy. After all, at that time China was still emerging from Maoism, Russia was in the Soviet Union, Brazil was a military dictatorship and India was constrained by the 'licence-permit Raj'. The supposed competitive threat from the 'BRIC' economies was muted at best.

Moreover, other major European economies saw no increase in income inequality in the 1980s. Income inequality in France has been stable for a prolonged period. In the Nordic countries income inequality has risen rapidly from a very low base since the middle of the 1990s, which still leaves the region as the most egalitarian in the world.

Wage stagnation began in the US in the 1970s, materialised in the UK in the 1990s, began to affect Germany in the early 2000s (fol-lowing a period of labour market deregulation) and only appeared in a very mild form in the Nordic world after the global crisis (Bailey et al. 2011). If there are no common patterns to the increase of income inequality or wage stagnation then it is hard to attribute these developments to a single global cause.

Varieties of capitalism

National institutions make an enormous difference to the experience of all of these phenomena. In other words, there are national variet-ies of capitalism that reflect national political choices. This story was first advanced in the early 2000s by Peter Hall and David Soskice who drew a distinction between liberal market economies (the UK and the US, for example) where markets are left to undertake the work of economic co-ordination and co-ordinated market economies (like Germany and Sweden) where institutions play a more important role (Hall and Soskice 2001). Both models deliver growth and prosperity but social outcomes are very different, with the US and Sweden at opposite ends of the spectrum of income inequality, for example.

Some commentators on the centre left in the pre-crisis period (not least the present author) emphasised the importance of political decisions in shaping economic and social outcomes. Lower levels of poverty and inequality in other developed economies demonstrated that the UK could make very different choices without any sacrifice in prosperity. Making Britain a little more like Germany could lead to higher productivity, a fairer capitalism and a robust tax base to support a more extensive range of public services.

Others drew a somewhat different conclusion, believing that the 'varieties of capitalism' story limited the range of choices available. In other words, policymakers had no alternative but to accept their inheritance. A liberal market economy was precisely that and any effort to reform the system along the lines of a co-ordinated market economy would do more harm than good (for a longer discussion see Sainsbury 2013).

Whether this argument is right or not is moot, not least because these economic models are the product of policy and business decisions made over long periods of time. They did not spring fully formed from policymakers' minds and may therefore be more malleable than the varieties of capitalism story suggests. Supposedly liberal market economies like the Republic of Ireland and Australia have used social pacts between government and trade unions to enforce wage restraint, implement economic reforms and boost productivity. Germany, as a 'co-ordinated market economy' has a low-pay problem that is very similar to the UK's. Levels of income inequality and the quality of employment are very different *within* the group of co-ordinated market economies – the Nordic countries, for example, have less low pay, higher-quality jobs and lower

income inequality than Germany (Gallie 2007, Coats 2013, Gallie
and Zhou 2013). Equally, before the Thatcherite reforms the UK
state played a rather more important role in the direct production of
goods and services and sought to take some responsibility for economic planning under governments of all political colours.[8]

Populism, immigration and identity

Today these arguments look rather less relevant than was the case
a decade ago. Most troubling for social democrats, perhaps, is that
rightwing populism is widespread no matter what variety of capitalism a country may have developed. Lower levels of poverty or
income inequality offer no insurance against the revival of reac-
tionary political forces. Far-right parties have witnessed significant
successes in countries with low unemployment and decent rates of
economic growth.

There can be no doubt that a politics of national identity has
witnessed a resurgence across the developed world, a phenomenon
that is often attributed to significant increases in migration and the
supposed impact on employment and wages. Once again, however,
there is a gap between the political narrative and the facts. No reputable economic study has been able to establish that recent levels of
migration have had any significant adverse impact on the job prospects or pay levels of native citizens. Another interpretation of the
hostility to immigration suggests the growth of the extreme right is
explained by cultural rather than economic concerns. It is said that
people are worried by foreign languages being spoken on the street,
the appearance of shops selling 'foreign' food or, most toxic of all,
the Islamisation of European societies.

We can be reasonably confident that some of the support for
nationalist parties is a consequence of straightforward racism or
hostility to 'the other'. But it seems implausible to argue that bigotry
alone is an adequate explanation. For example, the British Social
Attitudes Survey suggests that people are less likely to express
racial prejudice than was the case two decades ago. To understand

the recent course of events, we should, perhaps, return to our earlier analysis of the impact of capitalism and creative destruction on the ties that bind societies together.

The dangers for the centre left in responding inappropriately to the immigration question are clear. If we accept the view that an influx of 'foreigners' is the cause of populist discontent then we will develop policies to control immigration. But if there are deeper, structural factors explaining these anxieties then developing more restrictive immigration policies will make no difference whatsoever to the underlying problems. Certainly, there are questions of cultural confidence and identity that need to be considered in this context but the correct policy response may be some distance from these apparently cultural concerns. We need, therefore, to have some notion of how and why a politics of national identity becomes effective and what the centre left can do to respond without becoming mired in an unwinnable culture war.

The economist and philosopher Amartya Sen points out that in normal circumstances people are comfortable with multiple affiliations (Sen 2006). An individual can be a citizen of a particular nation, a member of a faith community, a parent or grandparent, join different political and civic associations, be a member of a trade union, work in a certain occupation, support a football club and have a range of extracurricular hobbies or interests. All of these elements are constitutive of an individual's identity. The acceptance of plural affiliations is the normal human condition; it makes us open to the world and able to have successful relationships with others. Acceptance of pluralism is an essential element of democracy too; without an understanding of difference, democracy, as a form of public reasoning, becomes impossible.

Identity is problematic, however, if one of the elements trumps or overwhelms all of the others. In Sen's view, anxiety about 'the other', about people who are different, is *abnormal* and results from a sense of grievance, loss and insecurity. Demagogues are able to exploit these anxieties for their own ends and the result is political violence.

Mercifully, the UK has been spared such extreme reactions since the Brexit referendum, but there has been much stigmatising of 'the other' and the tabloid press have been relentless in demonising both those who voted Remain and members of parliament who have the temerity to express scepticism about the consequences of leaving the EU. More seriously, perhaps, there is a question about whether rightwing newspaper editors genuinely accept the rule of law, with the *Daily Mail* in particular condemning judges as "enemies of the people", following the decision of the supreme court that the triggering of Article 50 required parliamentary approval. This satisfies at least one of Sen's conditions leading to violent outcomes – that the demands of the "sole" identity (in this case a peculiar notion of what it means to be a British patriot) are redefined in a particularly belligerent form.

This is where the nastiness creeps in (Sen 2006).

What makes this 'abnormal' use of identity possible? So far as Brexit and the rise of the far right across Europe is concerned, part of the answer may lie in the erosion of other elements of identity that, hitherto, had given people certainty and rootedness. In parts of the north of England, for example, the disappearance of industrial employment has eroded occupational identities secured through work. The same might be said for the decline in trade union membership, which both gave people a strong sense that there was a world beyond the confines of their immediate community, and emphasised the elementary democratic principle that not everybody would agree about everything all of the time – not least because there could be conflicts with both employers and other groups of workers, all of which had to be resolved through dialogue.

The importance of an industry to a town was not simply a matter of jobs. These activities made their own contribution to secure local identities – cotton in Lancashire, coal mining in south Wales, metal bashing in Birmingham, the potteries in Stoke-on-Trent – giving places distinctive cultures and personalities. Most importantly, these were confident and assertive identities, enabling people to say: 'this is the kind of person I am, this is where I stand and this is what I expect from life'. A feminist critic might say, correctly, that this all sounds very masculine – white male manual workers in secure jobs. But as the miners' strike of 1984–1985 proved, women played a critical role in the life of working-class communities. And from the 1960s onwards, women played an increasingly important role in the trade union movement, driving forward the campaign for equal pay and the removal of gender discrimination in employment.[9] Solidarity was not only of interest to men.

Moreover, for most of the twentieth century, working-class communities had a vibrant cultural life, with fairly equal participation across the sexes; there were thousands of largely self-educated people with an interest in art, literature and music, many of whom were committed to social progress through the labour movement (Rose 2001). And in the 1960s, of course, the wave of postwar social mobility brought people from working-class backgrounds to prominence in all of these fields. Whatever the privations to which these communities had been subjected in the past, there was a sense of possibility about the future.

One would struggle to make the same case today. 'Left-behind' communities are not characterised by cultural confidence. If you want a better job, a better house and a more comfortable life then the only option is to move. Many things that granted people respect and self-respect have been stripped away. Identity has been reduced from something complex to something simple – a crude idea about the nation, which is threatened by an influx of migrants – because the pluralistic elements of identity have died in the face of creative destruction.

Dispossessed communities are generally desperate to cling on to whatever they have. Change is seen as a threat. If economic opportunity is elusive then anything that might appear to upset the local social order, making things worse, is likely to be resisted. It is not too difficult to see how this syndrome can be exploited either by nationalist politicians of the extreme right or by charlatans who believe that playing the patriotic card is the fast track to leadership of the Conservative party.

Anthony Giddens has a rather inelegant expression which captures much of what has happened to communities that have failed to benefit from rising prosperity over the last 30 years: they are suffering from "ontological insecurity" (Giddens 1991). Expressed in less philosophical language, people make sense of their lives by developing a story about where they fit in the world; they are able to describe their experiences with a sense of continuity and order. But what if you cannot be certain about the nature of the world and your place in it? What if many of the features of life and work that you have taken for granted are no longer available either to you or to the rest of your community? What if the path through life that you foresaw for yourself and your children has been rudely curtailed? One can understand that in these circumstances there will be a search for someone to blame, for a simple explanation and for equally simple solutions.

Support for Brexit in many Labour-voting constituencies was, more than anything, a cry of protest, a howl of pain and an assertion that the economic and social status quo was unacceptable. People were making a simple statement: 'There is no solid ground on which I can stand, I blame immigrants and the EU, and I want to go back to the way things used to be'.

Nothing on offer from the Remain campaign could respond to these anxieties. David Cameron and George Osborne had little to say to communities under pressure except: 'You will be poorer if the UK leaves the EU'. On the one hand, this is nothing more than a statement of fact, but it did little to persuade those who believed they already had nothing to lose. Suggesting that EU membership would safeguard the UK's future prosperity proved unconvincing to communities more concerned about present or recent losses. In any event, many citizens in such communities believed that somebody else ('London', 'the south', 'the rich') would benefit from future prosperity whereas their prospects would be commensurately diminished. If the Labour campaign for Remain had been more dynamic, led by an enthusiastic rather than a timorous Jeremy Corbyn, then the result may have been different. In the circumstances, however, it is hardly surprising that many 'left-behind' voters decided to thumb their noses at the status quo.

One can see the same phenomenon across the EU. Identities crumbling in the face of economic restructuring, a revolt against elites, a turn to the far right and a cleaving to an exclusionary idea of nation as the only safe haven in a heartless and insecure world. The sense of dispossession, the belief that life for the next generation will be worse, the view that historic certainties have been swept from the stage all contribute to a profound feeling of unease. Perhaps the most important factor here is *loss*, a belief that the future will be worse than the past, that legitimate expectations are not being met, that somebody else is moving forward while I am standing still or sliding backwards.

The varieties of capitalism story tells us that some countries have done better than others on particular social and economic measures. But it offers little guidance for politicians seeking to understand how they respond to the rise of the populist right. What can be said with certainty is that none of the varieties of capitalism, as currently configured, offers the security demanded by many citizens. Some fundamental rethinking is required about how the risks created by market processes are to be managed and ameliorated.

PASOKIFICATION OR LEFTWING POPULISM?

The events of the last two years have compounded a dreadful decade for social democrats across Europe. Some parties, like PASOK in Greece, have been swept away completely by the backwash from the crisis and the rise of the leftwing populist party Syriza. The Dutch Labour party has witnessed its lowest vote share for a generation or more; the German SPD recorded a deeply disappointing performance in the most recent federal election; the Austrian Socialists are now in opposition, confronting a government that includes the

far-right Freedom party; and the French Socialists have been virtually eliminated from the political landscape by the rise of Emmanuel
Macron's progressive-centrist *En Marche!*. These are thin times for
social democrats across Europe.

One obvious question, therefore, is whether social democracy,
of the kind embraced by the present author, has permanently lost a
serious chance of winning power? It has been argued that the conditions that gave rise to social democracy are beginning to disappear
(Lawson 2016). The permanent, manual, skilled and semi-skilled
jobs that sustained organised labour are now on the wane. Trade
unions are less powerful everywhere. Ideas of solidarity, of shar-
ing risk and of common citizenship are increasingly ineffective, as
people rely on their own resources for security in an uncertain world.
And if people are looking for collective security, they find it in
exclusive notions of race, nation and community. Social democracy
cannot be sustained without social democrats, and there are simply
not enough social democrats around.

Another response is to say that all social democrats have to be
is patient. Eventually, the political cycle will turn, the right will
become unpopular and progressives will find themselves installed
in the chancelleries of Europe again. It would be foolish to rule this
argument out completely, but it carries very high risks and could be
seen as a recipe for complacency: 'social democracy isn't in crisis,
we don't need to change, we simply have to wait our turn'. Even if
this were true, it could prove to be a recipe for weak and ineffective government, not least because conventional social democratic
solutions have proved ineffective in offering genuine security in
difficult conditions of change and have led, indirectly, to the current
conjuncture. Micawberishly waiting for 'something to turn up', or
'one more heave' as we say in the UK, is not the most galvanising
of political strategies.

A third reaction is to say, 'yes, social democracy as conventionally conceived is finished, but look at the success of Jeremy
Corbyn's Labour (or Podemos, or Syriza) – there is real scope for
a radical leftwing populism that could transform the status quo'.

This volume is written in the belief that the left-populist stance offers a false prospectus, which could do more harm than good and, if an attempt were made to implement these policies by any government, could condemn that party to opposition for a generation. The fiscal realities in Greece have forestalled *all* of Syriza's radical ambitions. Jeremy Corbyn and John McDonnell would confront equally tragic fiscal policy choices were they to win a general election in the UK in the near future.

The real weakness of leftwing populism is that it makes no effort, in reality disavows any attempt, to prepare the electorate for the ruthless need to prioritise. Populism refuses to accept that there are real constraints on the capacity of governments to borrow (even for investment) or that politics is the art of the manageable compromise rather than a series of heroic victories, followed by a rousing chorus of cheers as the winner takes their lap of honour. Populism tells us that politics is easy, that all can have presents or prizes, that austerity can be ended at the stroke of the chancellor's pen and that, once a Labour government is installed, nothing will ever be difficult again. Leftwing populism is a determined ideological rejection of Aneurin Bevan's wise insight that the language of priorities is the religion of socialism.

So there is no cause for complacency and no reason to embrace the simplicities of populism, but there is no cause for inevitable despair either. The purpose of this volume is to demonstrate that social democracy is of enduring relevance to the advance of those values that western societies have held dear since the Enlightenment. Ensuring that all citizens have equal basic liberties along with the greatest possible quantity of practical freedom are the central ideological commitments of social democracy across Europe. Understanding populism is essential, but the response must not be itself populist. One might say that the success of Emmanuel Macron and *En Marche!* show that it is possible to construct a progressive electoral coalition in what otherwise seem to be hostile conditions. The best response for social democrats is a rigorous analysis of social realities, founded on fidelity to our values. The process will not be easy but the task is by no means impossible and the work must start now.

The question today, therefore, is whether democratic institutions can be restored as effective vehicles for participation and account-ability or whether the only possible future is a continuing erosion of trust in conventional politics and the irresistible rise of populism. Developing a compelling answer is a challenge for all mainstream politicians, from the centre right leftwards. For progressives, it demands much greater clarity about medium- and long-term goals, together with compelling answers to the following four questions:

Why is the world the way it is?
What is wrong with the world as it is?
What do we propose to do about it?
Why should the electorate trust us to make the right choices?

A resonant description of current realities must be followed by incisive analysis and a prescription that builds the trust required for electoral victory. But before we can address these practical matters there is a somewhat bigger question demanding an answer: why are we here, or, more precisely, what is the left's essential purpose?

WHAT IS LABOUR FOR?

It is surely time, then, to stop searching for fresh inspiration in the old orthodoxies and thumbing over the classic texts as though they could give oracular guidance for the future. The first need now, in R. H. Tawney's words, 'is to treat sanctified formulae with judicious irreverence and to start by deciding what precisely is the end in view".

Anthony Crosland, *The Future of Socialism* (1956)

THE POWER OF NOSTALGIA

There is a terrible tendency on the left to look to the past for inspiration, or worse, perhaps, to invoke some golden age when progressive politics was king, leaders were honest as well as effective and policies were both radical and practical. One interpretation of the narrative so far is that there is no need for new solutions. The problems confronting the nation are as old as capitalism itself – disruption of community life, the destruction of stable forms of employment, uncertainty and insecurity.

This, in slightly crude summary form, is the backward-looking case advanced by Ken Loach's film *The Spirit of '45*, celebrating the achievements of the postwar Labour government.

Loach's narrative displays the bold primary colours of socialist realism when the realities of the post-1945 period are better painted in shades of grey. The government was subject to continuing economic pressure, had to go cap in hand to the US for a substantial loan, fell out with the trade unions and compromised on the generosity of the insurance-based benefits offered by the welfare state. The *Keep Left* group in the parliamentary Labour party were emphatic in condemning the government's timidity and the failure to make sufficient progress towards the goal of a socialist society.

It is worth recalling too that Labour lost the 1951 election and failed to secure a majority again until 1964. The Attlee government was heroic in its own way, but by the early 1950s Labour was experiencing a period of profound existential angst. If thinkers in the mid-1950s, on both the right and left of Labour, felt that invoking the spirit of '45 was no recipe for victory then the same conclusion is certainly true today.

Enthusiasts for Jeremy Corbyn's leadership would suggest that there is no need to agonise about these questions. In their view, Corbyn has articulated Labour's purpose with some clarity during his two successful bids for the leadership and in the 2017 general election campaign. There can be no doubt that a large number of people were enthused by the possibility that there could be a radical alternative to the tired orthodoxy of Tory austerity and the compromises associated with New Labour. But Corbyn's speeches tended (and still tend) towards the general, with the principal rhetorical tropes emphasising Labour's commitment to the promotion and defence of peace, justice, equality and human rights. No doubt listeners understand the leader's intentions and are appropriately inspired by his material. But much of this language is about signalling virtue and does not offer a clear set of principles to distinguish Labour's approach from other political philosophies.

LABOUR'S DIVERSE IDEOLOGICAL TRADITIONS

This matters because purpose influences both narrative, the story a political party tells itself and the public about the world, and policy.

One might say that the Labour party has been experiencing an existential crisis in relation to fundamental purposes since its foundation. A good deal of ink has been consumed in answering the question, 'what is Labour for?'. Even those who have agreed that the fundamental objective is 'socialism' have disagreed about what is meant by the term. Labour's traditions are pluralist, diverse and in many cases quite contradictory. In the words of Anthony Crosland:

> *Fabian collectivism and Welfare Statism require a view of the State diametrically opposed to the Marxist view. The syndicalist tradition is anti-collectivist. The Marxist tradition is anti-reformist. Owenism differs fundamentally from Marxism and syndicalism on the class-war. Morrisite communes and Socialist Guilds are incompatible with nationalisation* (Crosland 1956).

As Crosland recognised, Marxism has made a distinctive contribution to Labour's thinking and many people on the left would accept a debt to Marx, including those who are not themselves Marxists. Nonetheless, the mainstream has consistently supported the notion that existing institutions can be used to secure enduring social change, with a socialist society brought into being using the normal machinery of government. Labour has never deviated from the parliamentary road.

The difference between orthodox Marxists and democratic socialists could, therefore, be described as an argument about means – revolution or reform – and it is certainly the case that there are serious thinkers in the democratic socialist tradition who believe that 'socialism' is an end point on the road of progressive advance (Crick 1984). This new social order represents a superior form of human civilisation because it will allow individuals to flourish fully. There will be no poverty, no inequality, no use of unaccountable power, no exploitation. In Bernard Crick's words, socialism is a doctrine and a theory:

> *The doctrine asserts the primacy and mutual dependence of the values of 'liberty, equality and fraternity', and it draws on the theory to believe that greater equality will lead to more co-operation than*

competition, that this will in turn enhance fraternity and hence liber-
ate from inhibition, restriction and exploitation both individual per-
sonality and the productive potential of society (Crick 1984).

More importantly, perhaps, democratic socialism on Crick's definition still betrays its roots in Marxist teleology. History is tending in
one direction, there is an end to the process and that end is 'socialism', at which point we can all declare 'job done' and presumably
leave the new social order to take care of itself.

This current of opinion has much in common with a similar
trope on the political right. After the end of the cold war, Francis
Fukuyama published *The End of History and the Last Man*, which
argued that all ideological contests were over; free markets and liberal democracy had won (Fukuyama 1992). For those with a teleological bent to their socialism the dilemma is clear. Fukuyama may
have been wrong about liberal democracy and the end of history.
But are democratic socialists just as guilty of hubris as some of their
opponents in believing that socialism, once established, will be an
immutable social order?

The best response to this challenge is to recognise that there are
other, equally important, streams of thought on the left, which seek
to get out of the teleological bind bequeathed to socialism by Marx.
Much of this thinking is derived from the work of Eduard Bernstein,
the pioneering German social democrat, whose *Evolutionary
Socialism* was published in 1899. His first question was: where is
the revolution? If Marx was right then the position of the working
class across industrialised societies ought to have been deteriorating.
In reality, the German working class had seen their incomes rising
not falling, trade unions were growing in membership and influence,
social democrats were making political progress and winning seats
in the imperial Reichstag. From the 1890s onwards the SPD won
a plurality of votes in the German empire, although the party was
always prevented from forming a government.

It was Bernstein who established the notion that bourgeois institutions like elections and parliaments could be instruments of social

progress. He also outraged most of his colleagues in the SPD by denying that there was any end state that socialists should be seeking.

> *What is generally called the ultimate goal of socialism is nothing to me. The movement is everything* (Bernstein 1899).

Bernstein had to proceed with care if he wanted to persuade sceptical colleagues. The extent of his radical revision of Marxism was hidden behind a rhetorical veil that allowed him to advance his argument without completely alienating all his readers.[1] Nonetheless, the clue is in the title of the book: *Evolutionary Socialism*. Obviously, there is a nod in the direction of Charles Darwin here. Evolution is counter-posed to revolution. But the most important point, which Bernstein left slightly obscure, is that evolution is not a teleological process leading to the appearance of an ideal or superior creature. Evolution is about random variation and adaptation, delivering an advantage for a species in the environment in which it finds itself; it is char-acterised by blind alleys, false starts and mass extinctions of previ-ously successful organisms. Political change is likely to be similar in nature, although the process is at least semi-conscious (because we are talking about human beings and institutions) rather than uncon-scious, lacking a direction or guiding hand (like evolution).

ETHICS AND VALUES: THE IMPORTANCE OF EQUALITY

So where does leave the politics of the left? To begin with we might say, following Bernstein, that political success requires a deep understanding of social realities. Political programmes are useless unless they are congruent with these realities, describe the world accurately and offer a practical, hopeful prospectus for change.

Second, the idea that the world can be remade according to a detailed ideological prescription should be abandoned.[2] Just because different worlds can be imagined does not mean that these worlds have any prospect of coming into existence. The experience of the last century should tell us that societies are complex and destroying one set of institutions does not guarantee the creation of a new set of superior institutions – just ask the citizens of Mao's China or Stalin's Soviet Union.

Third, we should reject the notion that history has a direction or purpose. There is no key to history as argued by orthodox Marxists and one cannot accelerate the process towards some inevitable historical end.[3]

Fourth, all those who identify as being on the left should stop talking about ultimate goals, final destinations or utopias. The people we seek to persuade do not think in these terms and we mislead them and ourselves in suggesting that there is some ideal society just beyond the horizon. Honesty and realism are cardinal virtues in the world of progressive politics.

At this point it might be wise to draw a clearer distinction between social democracy and democratic socialism. For the purposes of the remainder of this discussion I will use the expression social democracy to describe a left politics that rejects the notion of an end state called 'socialism' and I will use the expression democratic socialism to describe a politics still influenced by the legacy of Marxist teleology. Social democrats and democratic socialists have always had an uneasy relationship inside the Labour party and these differences, although not always explicitly articulated, produced the bitter doctrinal disputes during the 1950s, 1970s, 1980s and the period since Jeremy Corbyn's election in 2015.[4]

What unites both currents of thought is the high value placed on democracy, liberty and the ability of individual citizens to make choices, to exercise agency. Both social democracy and democratic socialism are concerned with the release of human potential in an environment of equal citizenship and accountable government, reflecting the importance of freedom, justice and fellowship. Inherent in this view is a protest against what Crosland called the "material poverty and physical squalor" produced by capitalism.

Other aspirations, on which democratic socialists and social democrats can agree include: a concern about social welfare, especially the relief of distress for those in need; a belief in equality and the "classless society", combined with a commitment to give workers their "just rights and responsible status at work"; a rejection of competitive antagonism and an ideal of fraternity and co-operation; and a protest against the inefficiencies of capitalism, especially the tendency of the system to create mass unemployment (Crosland 1956).

Morgan Phillips, a former general secretary of the Labour party, famously observed that Labour owed more to Methodism than Marxism. In part, this was a reflection of the importance of non-conformist churches in helping to create the organisational foundations on which the labour movement was built. Nonetheless, whether consciously or unwittingly, Phillips was reflecting something quite profound about the wellspring of Labour's values.

R. H. Tawney, for example, took it as axiomatic that the ethical basis of the case for equality is that we are all equal in the sight of God (Tawney 1931). Christianity provided the foundation on which Tawney developed his conception of social democracy. In this respect he is an exemplar of a particular current of English radicalism that emerged during the civil war, emphasising the importance of egalitarian, democratic citizenship.

In his famous speech from the scaffold in 1685, Richard Rumbold, who had been convicted of participation in a plot to assassinate Charles II, offered the following rallying call:

> *I am sure there was no man born marked of God above another, for none comes into the world with a saddle on his back, neither any booted and spurred to ride him.*

As a practical matter, therefore, status hierarchies are entirely human creations and they are in direct contradiction of 'nature' to the extent that some lives are given a higher value than others; the social position of parents is not deserved in any sense by their children.

All citizens should be treated as equal and that means having the right to participate in the governance of the nation.

Larry Siedentop, in a towering work of intellectual history, argues that much of what we now consider to be liberal thought has deep Christian roots (Siedentop 2015). Again, this is because all individuals are equal in the sight of God. But more than that, the notion of the individual as a conscious actor is derived, in part, from the idea that embracing Christianity is a matter of *individual conscience*. We are not to be judged according to our social status or our membership of a class, but according to those actions that either lead us to salvation or condemn us to damnation.

Once these notions of individual conscience and equality before God are established it becomes possible to make *comparisons*. If we are all God's creatures then why should some have the advantages of wealth and luxury while others starve? Why, in practice, should some lives be given a higher value than others? It is from this insight that we begin to derive notions of merit and desert, of just rewards and a strong intuition that excessive inequality is wrong, not least because it confers unequal power and status.

It is worth emphasising that while these values may be derived from theistic beliefs, they no longer depend for their effectiveness on faith in God. As Siedentop points out, apparently with some regret, the Enlightenment effectively secularised these values. The claims for equality, autonomy and participation are made simply by asserting membership of the human race.

By focusing on this ethical dimension, social democrats can avoid the weaknesses of Marxist system building. There is no need for a theory of history, no need to believe in a final consummation or transcendent experience, and no definitive commitment to particular means (socialisation of the means of production, for example) to achieve the ends that are sought. As society changes, so social democrats must look for new policy instruments. Political failure is inevitable if we either stop thinking or fail to pay close attention to the development of the economy and society.

How much and what kind of equality?

Crosland, in his revisionist account of British social democracy, emphasised the ends and means distinction to make the point that the expansion of public ownership, defined as the creation of more public corporations, would not necessarily lead to a more 'socialist' outcome. Attention had to be focused on the problems confronting a Labour government, which required a pragmatic or agnostic approach to the means to be used.

In Crosland's view the big problems confronting the country in 1956 were no longer a direct consequence of income inequality (he might think differently today of course) but of wider *social* inequalities. The emphasis was therefore on reducing social tension, what Crosland described as "the persistence of collective resentments", by acting on four fronts. First, by improving what we would now call life chances, principally by offering all children an equal chance of access to the best education available. Second, by taking action to reduce inherited wealth. Third, to break up concentrations of unaccountable power, with particular attention being paid to bureaucratic power in the workplace; Crosland was explicit that it must be a priority for a Labour government to increase the power of the worker at the point of production (Crosland 1956). Fourth, to seek a more equitable distribution of rewards from work, recognising that some people were paid too much and others paid too little. This did not mean that there should be a general levelling down, and incentives remained important, but Crosland believed that some limited compression of wages could be secured without any adverse effect on economic growth.

Readers unfamiliar with Crosland's thought could be forgiven for finding his approach a little unsatisfying. In response to the question 'how much equality?', he offers the following:

> [W]e need large egalitarian changes in our educational system, the distribution of property, the distribution of resources in periods of need, social manners and the style of life, and the location of power

within industry; and perhaps some, but certainly a smaller, change in
respect of incomes from work. . . . [T]hese changes, taken together,
will amount to a considerable social revolution (Crosland 1956).

No doubt Crosland was right to suggest that such reforms would
have a significant impact, but I would argue that he has failed to
give a sufficient answer to his own question. In particular, he goes
on to say that he has no idea where one might wish to stop on this
egalitarian journey; that is a matter for future generations. More
equality may be desirable today, but one cannot be certain whether
more equality will be desirable tomorrow.

Some social democrats have looked to John Rawls' monumental
A Theory of Justice as a potential answer to the 'how much equality?' question (Rawls 1971). At the time of its publication, Rawls'
masterwork was seen as offering a robust defence of egalitarian-
ism, building on sound philosophical foundations, consistent with
the Enlightenment belief (and the belief of some English Puritans)
that equality is the natural condition of human beings. Nonetheless,
despite the presumption of equality, some departures from the principle are to be permitted where those inequalities are to the benefit
of the least well-off in a society. In other words, to pursue equality beyond that point would be to the disadvantage of the poorest
citizens.

A serious difficulty arises, however, if one seeks to use *A Theory
of Justice* as a political manual rather than a philosophical treatise.
How can one know whether a particular level of inequality is to the
advantage of the poor or not? As an empirical matter, policymakers
with an egalitarian conviction can only answer this question once it
is clear that the citizens with the lowest incomes are worse off than
they were before the implementation of a particular policy initiative. Whether that structure of inequalities really is (or is not) to the
advantage of citizens with low incomes can only be judged *after* an
attempt has been made to reduce those inequalities.

Moreover, people of a conservative disposition might say that the
present structure of inequality *is* to the advantage of the poor and

any attempt to change the distribution will make everybody worse off; that, after all, is the justification for the trickle-down economics endorsed by Margaret Thatcher, Ronald Reagan and their successors. Rawls can be prayed in aid just as much by those who wish to cut taxes for the rich as those who wish to pursue a programme of egalitarian redistribution to benefit the poorest households.

At this point we need to enter a caveat in Rawls' defence. His first principle of justice is that all citizens must be guaranteed equal basic liberties – freedom to participate in the democratic process, freedom of speech, freedom of association, freedom of assembly – and these basic liberties can be threatened by excessive concentrations of income and wealth:

> *Disparities in the distribution of property and wealth that far exceed what is compatible with political equality have generally been tolerated by the legal system. . . . Moreover, the effect of injustices in the political system are much more grave and long-lasting than market imperfections. Thus inequalities in the economic and social system may soon undermine whatever political equality may have existed under fortunate historical conditions* (Rawls 1971).

Equality and liberty

The case for equality might be said to depend on the following related propositions. First, all citizens must be guaranteed equal basic liberties – Rawls' first principle of justice. Second, this principle is violated where money enables some people to make more use of their freedom than others by exercising a disproportionate influence over the governance of a society. Third, there is strong evidence to show that wide disparities of income and wealth have an adverse impact on the life chances of the poorest households – most notably in terms of general health and life expectancy (Marmot 2004). Fourth, excessive levels of income inequality are associated with economic crises on the scale of the Great Depression and the global crisis of 2007–2009 (Kumhof and Rancière 2010). Fifth, income inequality and lower levels of income redistribution are associated with lower levels of economic growth (Berg and Ostry 2010, Ostry et al 2014). Supporters of trickle-down economics are empirically mistaken – which, recalling Alan Greenspan's comments on the failure of the pre-crisis paradigm, is not entirely surprising.

Equality is important, therefore, not as an end in itself but as an *instrumental* value.[5] It helps both individuals and societies to achieve other objectives. We could describe that objective as 'liberty' or 'freedom' but a more detailed definition might be useful. Most importantly, perhaps, the end in view here is to ensure that citizens are empowered to take control of their lives, to make decisions that matter, be masters of their fate and, in a resonant phrase to which we will have cause to return, possess the capabilities they need to choose lives they have reason to value.

Of course, some conservatives would argue that they have their own conception of liberty, which, at risk of some distortion, is constituted by an absence of state control of economic life and the freedom to earn as much as you can, spending whatever you can, in any way you choose. Freedom, on this conception, consists almost entirely in the capacity to undertake "capitalist acts between consenting adults" (Nozick 1974). One might even say that, on this view, freedom amounts to little more than accumulating wealth and shopping – which is not quite what the Enlightenment *philosophes* had in mind.

Social democrats, on the other hand, are preoccupied with another question: just how much practical freedom does our society offer its citizens? Or, for those of a more Rawlsian tendency, to what extent does our society really guarantee all citizens equal basic liberties? A constitutional guarantee of free speech is of little interest to somebody who is starving or illiterate. Barriers to full social participation based on gender, race, sexuality or religion self-evidently prevent people from taking command of their lives. Social democracy is best defined, perhaps, as a conception of freedom that is serious about giving citizens real power – which is why the ability of right-wing populists to purloin the phrase 'take back control' is so galling. Nonetheless, there is a lesson for the left in that too.

Whatever Labour and other social democratic governments have done across the developed world in the last 30 years, they have not managed to create an inclusive, resilient society where *all* citizens believe they are participants in a shared enterprise rather than victims of forces beyond their control. To that extent, some of the vices of laissez-faire capitalism,[6] far from being eliminated, continue to prove a source of social conflict.

If any conservatives have managed to read this far they will no doubt be dredging from the back of their minds Isaiah Berlin's distinction between "negative freedom" and "positive freedom" in the hope that they can stop these pesky social democrats in their tracks (Berlin 1969). Berlin's essay, *Two Concepts of Liberty*, has often been read as an explicit rejection of ideologies across the left spectrum, from reformist social democracy to the wilder shores of Trotskyism.

Berlin appears to suggest that the only freedom that matters is "negative freedom" or the absence of coercion. "Positive freedom", on the other hand, encompasses some notion of "self-mastery", to be a subject not an object:

> *I wish to be somebody, not nobody; a doer – deciding, not being decided for* (Berlin 1969).

The proper role of the state, on one interpretation of this view, is to do little more than protect negative freedom. The conclusion is clear: there is no case for an expansive state, high taxes or persistent worrying away at the 'how much equality?' question. So long as the state keeps out of the way, a people can be said to be free.

Berlin's concern, however, is to attack those notions of positive freedom, most obviously some Marxist conceptions, which allow for the abrogation of the bourgeois freedoms (Rawls' basic liberties) in pursuit of some "higher" ideal of "genuine" freedom – the liberation of the working class from oppression, the transition to a socialist society, or (to take a Leninist stance) the acceleration of the historical process by a vanguard party towards the inevitability of communism. To express the same point slightly differently, moving towards a better world of "real" freedom might require an absolute prohibition of "capitalist acts between consenting adults", which seems inconsistent with the principle that citizens should be able to undertake these capitalist acts if they genuinely wish to do so.

It is fair to say, perhaps, that conservatives (and some social democrats) have taken Berlin more than a little literally and have failed to do justice to the complexity of his argument. Most importantly, perhaps, he explicitly rejects the notions of both laissez-faire and the minimal state, referring to the "brutal violations of negative liberty" associated with unconstrained free markets.

Freedom for the wolves has often meant death to the sheep (Berlin 1969).

In other words, poverty, a denial of citizenship in the workplace and discrimination on the grounds of gender, race, sexuality or ethnicity are all forms of coercion, violating negative liberty. Berlin's conception is entirely consistent with the idea of a regulatory state which prohibits child labour, establishes employment rights, encourages the development of collective bargaining, fixes health and safety standards and protects the environment.

The distinction between "positive" and "negative" freedom is expressed by Berlin with great clarity, but the differences are subtle. What many conservative commentators have failed to notice, perhaps having been swept along by Berlin's bravura critique of some conceptions of Marxism, is that *power* and *capability* are central to the idea of negative liberty.

For what use are rights without the power to implement them? (Berlin 1969).

Coercion does not have to be explicit or directly oppressive. Class, income, the rigging of educational policies, the legislative enforcement of social norms[7] or the presence of exclusive social networks can all create barriers that impede "negative freedom". It is quite wrong to interpret Berlin as an enthusiast for what some might now describe as neo-liberalism and what, hitherto, would have been described as laissez-faire.

> *The extent of a man's [sic] negative liberty is, as it were, a function of what doors are open to him; upon what prospects they open; and how open they are* (Berlin 1969).

The argument in *Two Concepts of Liberty* should, therefore, be read as meaning that a particular interpretation of Marxism (more accurately Leninism) is a threat to freedom. It is quite wrong, however, to interpret Berlin's account as a decisive argument against the claim that social democracy is, fundamentally, about liberty too.[8]

For the purposes of this discussion, the distinction between positive and negative liberty is important because it enables us to be more precise about the nature of the social democratic commitment to freedom. It equips us with an effective critique of revolutionary philosophies and vanguard parties. Moreover, it also means that we can have an honest discussion about what happens when the claims of liberty and equality conflict.

For example, it might be argued that the existence of a public school-educated elite in the UK undermines the value of equal citizenship because a relatively narrow social group have a grip on both money and power. An egalitarian, looking to tackle the problem at the root, could seek either to abolish the public schools entirely or require them to act as genuine charities so that access depended on academic ability rather than the wealth of a child's parents. A standard conservative response to this case is that any assault on the public schools is an abrogation of freedom. People should be at liberty to spend their money as they choose and if this means buying an exclusive education for their children then they should be able to do so.

One cannot simply 'read off' the right answer to this question from Berlin's account of negative liberty, but nor can one simply say the conservative argument is decisive. The most important point here is that there must be a public conversation about where the balance should be struck between the freedom of parents to buy their children's education and the rights of all to be treated as equal citizens.

If freedom for the wolves often does mean death to the sheep then the upshot of Berlin's argument is that action must be taken to restrain the predatory instincts of those who, although they might benefit from the operation of the economic and social system, do a great deal of harm to others as a result. There is no right answer about where the necessary lines should be drawn. But that is why democracy, the process of public discussion, matters so much. The national conversation about where the balance is to be struck between competing values is perpetual. One might even say that this is the real meaning of pluralist democracy – that we can, as a society, have the argument and reach a decision that is viewed as legitimate, even by those who did not prevail, and who live to fight another day.

The account given so far has been impeccably liberal, but a sceptical reader may be asking themselves, what is social democratic about this discussion of freedom? Surely, social democrats are in favour of collective action to liberate whole classes of people, not the liberation of individuals from constraints and the conferring of individual rights? Where is the 'social' element in this story?

A natural response is to say that even Marx was concerned with the liberation of individuals, albeit as a result of the revolutionary action of the proletariat.

In communist society, where nobody has one exclusive sphere of activity but each can become accomplished in any branch he wishes, society regulates the general production and thus makes it possible for me to do one thing today and another tomorrow, to hunt in the morning, fish in the afternoon, rear cattle in the evening, criticise after dinner, just as I have a mind, without ever becoming hunter, fisherman, herdsman or critic (Marx 1845).

Leaving aside the implausibility of the vision, Marx is making the simple point that the range of choices available to individuals will be much wider after the revolution. There can be no doubt too that it is *autonomous individuals* doing the choosing. We are worlds away from an authoritarian state or a Stalinist approach to the management of labour.

What distinguishes social democrats from liberals is the commitment to collective action, the belief that only by working together can we create the conditions of our own freedom; or, in the words of the Labour party constitution, "by the strength of our common endeavour we achieve more than we achieve alone". As with equality, collective action is an *instrument* of emancipation:

> *Collective action is the means. Individual rights are the object – individual rights when properly defined as their extension to the largest possible number of citizens, and the provision, for those citizens, of the ability to make the theoretical rights a practical reality"* (Hattersley 1987).

Collective action is also necessary to address other inequalities of power that prevent equal citizenship from being realised in a capitalist society, most notably in the workplace. One of social democracy's central commitments is that people do not surrender their rights as citizens at the point they cross their employer's threshold. This means that the basic liberties (freedom of speech, freedom of association) are just as relevant at work as they are in civil society. There is an obvious inequality of power between the individual worker and the employer, which by definition is a collective entity. The employer has the power to hire and fire, the worker simply has the opportunity to look for another job. A belief in industrial democracy, in giving people real control over their working lives, demands support for worker participation in the process of decision making, rights for trade unions to organise and the endorsement of collective bargaining as a collective good for both workers and employers. Unless these steps are taken then freedom for the wolves in the labour market really does mean death to the sheep.

What kind of equality?

So far, however, we have failed to give a precise answer to the 'how much equality?' question, settling instead on the not entirely satisfactory formulation that society would be better with a good deal less inequality than exists today. Another way to address the issue is to consider exactly *what kind* of equality matters if the goal is to enhance the sphere of practical freedom.

During the ascendancy of New Labour the commitment to equality was often parsed as a commitment to equality of opportunity. A good example of this line of thought can be found in Gordon Brown's introduction to the 2006 edition of Crosland's *The Future of Socialism*:

> Crosland would [if he were writing in the early 2000s] *have focused on the potential of every individual. He would have made a sharper distinction between equality of opportunity where he would have favoured a radical and expansive view of opportunity and equality of outcome. He would have probably talked more about equal opportunities and fair outcomes* (Brown 2006).

Nonetheless, this conception of equality is not entirely unproblematic. To begin with, the idea of "equality of opportunity" does nothing to subject the existing structure of inequalities to critical scrutiny. It can be interpreted, quite reasonably, as the equal opportunity to become unequal, even if those inequalities that do exist undermine the equal value of the basic liberties for all citizens.[9] There is a reason why some Conservatives are perfectly comfortable with the idea of equality of opportunity, particularly if it is defined in purely formal terms – where there are no explicit, legal barriers preventing individuals from making progress in their lives. In this sense, equality of opportunity means little more than a career open to talents.

Alternatively, a genuine commitment to "equality of opportunity" could require a very intrusive state, which sought to correct at every moment of an individual's life for inequalities created by class, income, gender, sexuality, access to social networks or brute luck. The state would need to be eternally vigilant in eliminating the slightest suggestion of disadvantage that limited "opportunity". To express the argument somewhat crudely, equality of opportunity is either banal, or illusory or authoritarian.

Social mobility is related to the idea of equality of opportunity. It has its roots in the belief that people with talent or ability should be able to transcend their backgrounds, climb the social ladder and secure a higher position in a status hierarchy. Of course, there is nothing objectionable about allowing individuals to fulfil their potential; one might say that this is the central purpose of social democracy. But inherent in the arguments for social mobility are the ideas of 'escape', 'moving on' and 'moving up'. Again, the existing structures of inequality are accepted, so long as those at the bottom of the pyramid have a decent shot at reaching the top. Much of the discussion of social mobility assumes an inexorable upward movement, but the corollary of upward mobility for some must be downward mobility for others. This is not necessarily an attractive vision of the social order. Or, to put the argument somewhat differently, if policymakers focus on generating upward movement they may devote less attention than is required to ensuring that those at the bottom (and who stay there) have lives rising above the level of the relentlessly awful.[10]

More dedicated egalitarians have suggested that the end in view should be equality of outcome, so that all citizens find themselves in broadly the same position: equal incomes, equal wealth, equal life chances (Tawney 1931). On this measure, Tawney, as an enthusiast for equal outcomes, was offering a more radical prospectus than anything that can be found in Crosland (or Rawls for that matter). Crosland was quite clear: economic incentives matter and some inequalities of income will continue even if social inequality, the visible difference between classes in manners and styles of life, is reduced.

The philosopher Ted Honderich, in his lengthy critique of conservatism, observes that one of the few rightwing arguments with

real power is the rejection of "equality of result" on the grounds of
irrationality. Tawney's case appears to be that equality, defined in
these terms, is to be pursued because it will ensure that all citizens
have equally satisfying lives. But it seems perverse to follow the
argument to its logical conclusion since one would, on this view,
prefer a poor but egalitarian society over a society characterised by
greater inequality in which *everybody* was better off (Honderich
2005). We may speculate that Tawney meant something else entirely
by equality of result, but, for the purposes of this discussion, where
Tawney is unable to speak for himself, the only conclusion one can
draw is that equality of result is no more attractive as an ideal than
equality of opportunity.

The idea that the accumulation of wealth must be *for* something
has a venerable pedigree – it was an argument first advanced by
Aristotle and, most recently, has been developed by the economist
and philosopher Amartya Sen as a principle that supports the case
for economic growth as a route to the expansion of practical liberty
for citizens (Sen 1999, Sen 2009). At one level this is little more
than a straightforward, common sense idea. The process of development since the industrial revolution has seen huge improvements
in human welfare. Medical science has eliminated infectious diseases and developed treatments for acute conditions, labour-saving
devices in the home have liberated women from domestic drudgery,
technological change has reduced the necessity for back-breaking
manual labour. To that extent it is obvious that development is associated with the expansion of freedom. Technological development
and the ability of individuals to choose lives that they have reason
to value have enjoyed a symbiotic relationship.

More importantly, for Sen, freedom depends on individuals
achieving certain "functionings" that depend on the possession of
particular "capabilities". A wide range of inequalities can create barriers; to this extent Sen's conception of freedom is consistent with
the account we have given of Berlin's argument that some features
of uncontrolled capitalism constitute a form of coercion. In other
words, inequality has an adverse effect on capability. Our attention

here is drawn to more than just inequalities of income; race, gender, sexuality and faith can be just as important. It is quite possible, therefore, to envisage a society characterised by much less income inequality than the UK has today, where life chances or capabilities are limited by these other disadvantages.

Examining capability and practical freedom also enable us to develop effective benchmarks for progress. Simply raising a household's income to £1 above the poverty level is a social policy achievement of a sort; it will reduce poverty in formal terms and may also modestly reduce income inequality, depending of course on what is happening to top incomes. But it does little to enlarge the sphere of practical freedom for that household. To that extent, social democrats have failed to develop effective instruments measuring whether theoretical rights have been made practical reality.

LABOUR'S DOCTRINAL DISPUTES

An open, questing, restless spirit is central to any kind of effective leftwing politics and should, in principle, allow for comradely disagreement. One is driven away from the mindset that there is one true social democratic faith in favour of a serious discussion between people with shared values.

Anybody with even a sketchy understanding of the Labour party's doctrinal disputes over the last 40 years may find this an absurdly idealistic account. In the early 1980s, Tony Benn and his followers acted as if they were the only authentic keepers of the flame. If one felt uncomfortable with the strictures of the Bennite left then the only option was to exit Labour rightwards and join the SDP. Under Tony Blair's leadership, some of his supporters viewed even mild criticism of 'the project' as a hallmark of disloyalty, meaning that mainstream social democrats could be depicted as dangerous Trots. Both wings of the party ran the risk that a constructive conversation in a broad church was sacrificed in favour of a cultish level of exclusivity. It is not too fanciful to suggest that a similar dynamic is at work today, as over-enthusiastic Corbynistas seek to root out 'red Tory' or 'Blairite' heresies.

Disagreements about doctrine generally surfaced following defeat in a general election, caused deep divisions and condemned the party to opposition for long periods (1951–1964, 1979–1997, 2010 onwards). Both left and right believed that their factional victory was essential if the party were to be saved as a viable electoral force. In reality, however, these profound differences played out as a zero-sum game; there was certainly one winner and one loser, but overall the party was no better off, and went on to suffer a series of further general election defeats.

Arguably, Labour had made a rod for its own back by failing to bring rhetoric and reality into alignment. There was an inevitable tension between the language of socialist transformation and the practicalities of governing in an essentially capitalist society where Labour was not going to nationalise every last corner shop or wholly reject the usefulness of markets. One might even go so far as to say that the leadership were deliberately misleading the membership, with bold promises of socialism weakly reflected in the necessary compromises and tragic choices of progressive governance. Disappointment amongst members was unavoidable; Labour governments would always fall short.

What can best be described as the betrayal myth is a somewhat unhelpful standpoint from which to view the world and it prevents the party, with its hugely increased membership, from developing a clear understanding of its history, including an accurate description of what happened to secure the election victories in 1964 and 1997 following long periods of Tory government.

In the 1980s, for example, the problem confronting the party was the resurgence of an initially broad-based left, which had its roots in a reaction to the disappointments of the Wilson and Callaghan governments. Once again this was wrapped in a myth of betrayal – that these governments had 'sold out' and made inadequate progress towards socialism. The solution was to democratise the party by subjecting MPs to a process of mandatory reselection.[11] If an MP resiled from the manifesto or failed to compel the government to implement a socialist programme, they ought to know that their constituency party could get rid of them, finding a replacement amongst the ranks of true believers.

Many of those supporting this stance claimed Marxist roots, which is more than a little curious, since the whole analysis depended upon the belief that Labour governments had failed in the past because the wrong people were in control. Change the personnel and you change the context, ensuring that transformational rhetoric and practical action are consistent. On this view, the way to get more socialism was to get more authentic socialists into parliament.

The other approach to reconciling rhetoric and reality has been to drop the language of transformation and accept the fact that Labour is and has always been a reformist party, committed to parliamentary institutions. One reading of Hugh Gaitskell's effort to revise clause IV in 1959–1960 is that only by changing the Labour party's constitution could aspiration and political practice be adequately reconciled. The same can be said for Tony Blair's successful campaign to rewrite clause IV in 1995, although in that case the constitutional revision was as much about the remaking of Labour's image ("New Labour, New Britain") as it was about a serious philosophical reflection on Labour's essential purpose. It is possible to go further and say that, far from being a fundamental ideological reorientation of the party, New Labour just did not go far enough in being honest about the kind of party it sought to become. As Philip Gould observed at the time, the revolution was unfinished (Gould 1999).

At this point it is important to be clear. I am not arguing that New Labour should have been even more enthusiastic in embracing the pre-crisis status quo – quite the reverse in fact. New Labour should have affirmed the egalitarian commitments described above at the same time as it rejected any notion of end states, ideal societies or immutable new social orders. An instructive comparison is with the abandonment of Marxism by the SPD at its Bad Godesberg convention in 1959. Any references to particular means were deleted from the constitution, a commitment to equal citizenship was installed as the operational principle and combined with the notion of "as much [of the] market as possible, as much [of the] state as necessary".

Labour's supposed ideological revolution under Blair was more modest. The new clause IV contains the words "Labour is a democratic socialist party", a formula that is best described as studiedly ambiguous. One can understand the realpolitik that influenced Blair and his colleagues – there was a need to keep the Labour coalition together and a frontal assault on those who retained a romantic attachment to 'socialism' could have been fatal to the case for reform.

The seeds of Corbynism were sown at precisely the moment that Blair abandoned the process of ideological modernisation. One can see that the prime minister was less than convinced by the extent of the change he had wrought. Policymaking became increasingly centralised in Downing Street as the years in government passed. In principle, the party's new policymaking machinery could have led to more genuine member involvement – the National Policy Forum, its subsidiary regional bodies and policy commissions should have allowed for deliberative discussion that was superior to the old resolutionary socialism of composite motions cobbled together for consideration by the annual conference. The reality was rather different: policy was developed in No 10 and then presented to the party for ratification, albeit that the trade unions retained some leverage to get their preferred commitments into the manifesto.

Before we turn to the possibilities for the future, it is worth recording that Labour wins elections when the party is united and has a convincing programme that matches the spirit of the times. This was certainly true in 1945, when the manifesto enjoyed broad-based support across the party. It was true in 1964, when Harold Wilson's careful temporising brought right and left together around a programme of technological modernisation to be delivered by "planning" – albeit that leading Labour figures disagreed about what planning might mean. It was true too in 1997, when Blair enjoyed the enthusiastic support of what, in the 1980s, had been known as the soft left. The critical point is that successful Labour leaders have recognised the party's pluralist traditions and have sought to avoid the imposition of doctrinal uniformity. There is a serious question whether Jeremy Corbyn, or at least a significant minority of his aco-lytes, have understood this very simple lesson.

POSSIBILITIES FOR THE FUTURE

The party is some distance from this culture today, with various factions suggesting that their preferred prescription is the only route to electoral success. Options are to be closed down, not opened up, and some elements on the left appear determined to impose a new orthodoxy on a broad-based party. Essentially, the party is being offered four choices: continued Corbynism; a reliance on the transformative power of technology to usher in a new social order; a focus on the socially conservative tendency in Labour's tradition; and, a revival of New Labour-style centrism.

Each of these possibilities will be assessed against the four questions posed at the end of Chapter 1. To what extent do these lenses accurately explain what is happening in the world? Is an adequate account given of the problems that Labour ought to be addressing? Are the policy proposals well matched to these challenges? How does each approach propose to convince the electorate that Labour can be trusted to make the right judgements?

Continued Corbynism

Jeremy Corbyn has now led the Labour party for almost three years and, in normal circumstances, it ought to be possible to set out the leader's policy prospectus in some detail. Moreover, one should be able to describe this agenda in a coherent ideological framework and give a detailed account of the ambitions of a Corbyn-led government.

Certainly, we know from his two leadership campaigns and the general election manifesto that Corbyn is opposed to 'austerity'; but that is a slogan rather than a policy. Equally, we know that the current leadership believes that the economy is rigged against ordinary people, although this is rather thin gruel when judged against the expansive policy agenda promoted by the supporters of Tony Benn in the 1980s.

During that period, the left had an analysis of the failures of British capitalism, founded on the argument that persistent under-investment had led to falling productivity growth and declining incomes relative to other major economies. On this view Britain could not be regenerated without a significant extension of public ownership, the imposition of compulsory planning agreements on those companies that remained in the private sector and big increases in public spending to improve the quality of health and social services. It was recognised that that an expansionary fiscal policy (more borrowing and spending) could just suck in imports, so import controls were proposed to ensure that the stimulus was restricted to the domestic economy. Just as with John McDonnell's recent 'war-gaming' of a run on the pound, exchange controls would have been necessary to prevent capital flight. Progress towards socialism required something close to a siege economy. The Bennite left's story in the 1970s and 1980s represented a serious effort to answer at least the first three of our four questions, even though it fell at the hurdle of practicability and failed to win the electorate's trust.

Nothing like this is available from Corbyn or McDonnell today. Far from offering a resonant analysis of the country's problems, the 2017 manifesto is better viewed as a straightforward exercise in populist, retail politics. The policies may have been popular, but they lacked both narrative and ideological coherence and offered little guidance as to how Labour would manage the inevitable compromises of progressive governance. For example, the proposal to abolish tuition fees proved very attractive, but was principally a big tax cut for middle-class households. It was also very expensive and would have cost the exchequer £11 billion, resources that might, for example, have been devoted to improving the life chances of children in disadvantaged communities.

At the same time, Labour said nothing about restoring the cuts to benefit levels implemented by the Tories. As Andrew Harrop has persuasively argued, Labour's policies, over the life of a parliament, would have seen middle-class incomes rising and the incomes of the poorest households falling (Harrop 2017). In other words, poverty would have been both wider and deeper after five years of Labour government. It is one thing to make speeches about the need to address income inequality and apparently quite another to adopt policies that will make a serious difference to those with barely enough money to make ends meet.

McDonnell claimed that the manifesto pledges were fully costed. Labour's additional spending would be paid for by higher taxes for the most affluent, a financial transactions tax, increases in corporation tax and a crackdown on tax avoidance. There can be no doubt that the approach was more rigorous than the wholly uncosted Conservative manifesto but, as the Institute for Fiscal Studies pointed out, Labour was not offering a fully funded package either (IFS 2017). The proposed tax rises would not have produced the projected revenue, there would have been a shortfall in the receipts from the clampdown on tax avoidance and the increase in corporation tax would have raised less revenue than anticipated in the long run. If Labour wanted to fund the manifesto pledges and, at some stage, restore the Conservatives' benefit cuts, then the only option would have been to borrow more. More seriously, perhaps, no account was taken of the likely impact of Brexit on the public finances, where the best evidence available (the government's leaked impact assessment) forecasts slower growth and lower tax receipts. Labour was proposing the highest level of public spending since the 1980s without offering a clear idea of how these commitments would be funded.

Mario Cuomo, the former governor of New York, was renowned for saying that you campaign in poetry and govern in prose. Once in office hard choices cannot be avoided by windy rhetoric or the expression of general goodwill. 'Niceness', avuncularity or even being 'the Absolute Boy' will not make it any easier to deal with the dilemmas of progressive governance. Today, Corbynism describes an unfair world in terms many people can understand, but the policies are poorly matched either to the description of the problems or to the ambitions of social transformation. And if policies are ill-considered, or populist rather than workable, then the party will struggle to win the trust of sceptical voters.

In a spirit of generosity, the best one might say for Labour's new establishment is that it is asking some of the right questions about the world but identifying very few of the right answers. Perhaps this is simply a reflection of inexperience. If the first part of wisdom is recognising one's own weaknesses then the current leadership should accept that there are many people from other currents of opinion in the party with relevant expertise. Developing a successful manifesto in 2022 and sustaining those policies in government demands the engagement of more than the small coterie currently responsible for Labour's ideas. One might even say that Corbyn and his colleagues are at risk of falling into the 'Blairite' trap of believing that only they are the authentic custodians of virtue and that there is nothing to be gained from open, honest, pluralist discussion. To emphasise once again, both the left and right of the party have been guilty of this approach in the past and, in the long run, it has done nothing but harm to Labour's prospects.

The transformative power of technology

The second lens through which we are invited to view the world focuses on the transformative power of technology. This comes in an optimistic and pessimistic variant. The optimistic scenario suggests that the rise of intelligent machines will render the logic of capitalist accumulation impossible. Goods will be produced at low or zero cost, making profits elusive. The automation of almost all productive activity will mean that nobody will need to work. During a transitional period, before the new order is established, those who lose their jobs or have their hours reduced by automation will need to be supported by a universal basic income (UBI), available to all citizens, funded by a tax on the excess profits of the giant tech companies. The pessimistic scenario is essentially the same initial story, with a very different ending. All jobs are set to disappear as the machines take over. A small number of plutocrats who own the machines will be the only beneficiaries, making super-profits. At this point the stories converge to the extent that, in the pessimistic narrative, the only way to forestall a revolution is to offer the dispossessed a UBI, funded by taxes on the excess profits of the tech giants.

Whether the 'end of work' story has any credibility at all is dealt with at length in the next chapter. The remainder of this discussion is focused on the political economy that justifies the optimistic scenario about our likely future and considers whether the left can rely on a kind of technological determinism to do much of the political heavy-lifting associated with the creation of a more egalitarian society.

Developing this argument requires a short detour down the byways of Marxist theory. We have already noted that Bernstein asked the simple question "where is the revolution?" at the end of the nineteenth century. 60 years later some Marxists had become increasingly disillusioned with the unwillingness of the proletariat to fulfil its revolutionary destiny. Herbert Marcuse in *One Dimensional Man*, for example, argued that the working class had been anaesthetised by the success of social democracy (the welfare state and full employment) and the seductions of consumerism (Marcuse 1964). Working people were so satisfied with their lives that they had ceased to understand the exploitative nature of the system to which they were subject. Under these conditions the revolution as predicted by Marx would prove impossible. Social progress depended on minorities and marginalised groups, working outside normal political channels for radical social change.

Paul Mason, in his account of technology and the future of capitalism, draws on some of this thinking to suggest that a strange new constellation of intelligent machines, the Occupy protestors, leftwing populist parties and the open source movement will usher in a new social order. Class struggle and the victory of the proletariat may no longer be the key to history, but capitalism is still riven with contradictions, will experience an inevitable decline in the rate of profit, is destined to experience some final crisis and will be replaced by a new form of "postcapitalism" (Mason 2015). Technology, rather than the proletariat, becomes the agent of historical transformation. The difficulty with this analysis, of course, is that it falls prey to the illusion that the future is predictable, that capitalism is doomed to collapse (we have been waiting for this since at least 1848) and that there is some end state we can only describe as a better world.

Despite these weaknesses, what Mason diagnoses, with both accuracy and passion, are the corruptions of finance-driven capitalism, the baleful consequences of income inequality and the disruption to settled patterns of life and work associated with technological upheaval. To that extent, all he has done is affirm Schumpeter's account of creative destruction. But policymakers would be ill-advised to believe that *Postcapitalism* is either a handbook for political victory or an accurate guide to the likely course of events.

A more nuanced version of the story is that technology will allow for big reductions in working time because of rapid productivity growth. This is a more respectable argument. J. M. Keynes, for example, in *Economic Possibilities for our Grandchildren*, suggested that by the end of the twentieth century nobody would need to work for more than 15 hours each week (Keynes 1931). Even the least attentive student of economics will understand that we are still waiting for this remarkably short working week to materialise. Productivity may have risen since the early 1930s, but full-time working hours remain stubbornly stuck in the 35 to 40 zone.

One might therefore dispense with the case for the UBI by simply saying that the analysis on which it is based – rising technological unemployment leading to a world without work – is tendentious at best. If there will be an adequate number of jobs available in the future then the focus should be on achieving decent incomes for all those who work, not taxing the owners of the robots and redistributing the proceeds through the UBI.

The social democratic commitment to liberty is also relevant in this context. We have always believed in the power of collective action to liberate individuals. The case for independent trade unionism rests on this principle, with organised labour acting to ensure the fairest possible distribution of wages before the intervention of the state through the tax and benefit system – this is what Ed Miliband meant when he talked about predistribution (Coats 2013). Advocates of the UBI, wherever they may be located on the political spectrum, are denying the possibility that workers can have any collective influence over their level of earnings. The UBI and independent trade unionism make at best uncomfortable and at worst wholly contradictory bedfellows.

As a practical matter, implementing the UBI is only possible following a comprehensive redesign of the welfare state and a complete recasting of the relationship between social security and work. There is no guarantee that the consequence of this radical upheaval will be a significantly superior system. Nor is it likely that the UBI will secure the confidence of the electorate, principally because it is unrelated to contribution and is entirely unconditional. The Conservative party has proved that low politics can work; that stigmatising those in receipt of benefits as lazy, feckless and unworthy of support is an effective line of attack against Labour. If we are serious about making the case for the welfare state then the left must argue for a contribution-based system of social security, with additional resources available to those who cannot work and who will never acquire an entitlement to contributory benefits. Devoting an excessive level of attention to the UBI will divert Labour from this more important task.

What might be crudely characterised as the technological determinist narrative has certainly created interest amongst the chattering classes, but it is less compelling as a political diagnosis than the story promoted by supporters of Corbyn. The real value of Mason's account is that he draws our attention to the importance of creative destruction and the need to give people security in conditions of uncertainty. We would be foolish to ignore his insights, even if we reject his overconfident predictions about the future. Beyond that, *Postcapitalism*, while undeniably interesting, does not offer an adequate answer to our four questions and, in advocating the UBI, could lead the Labour party in a politically dangerous direction.

Blue Labour

Reference has already been made to Labour's conservative tendency, the most articulate expression of which in recent times has been Maurice Glasman's development of that set of ideas known as Blue Labour (Davis 2011). The principal concern here is that the Labour party has lost touch with its working-class base and must develop a strategy that appeals to people who value rootedness, community, predictability and security over cosmopolitanism, globalisation, novelty or the changes wrought by unregulated markets. Blue Labour is often described as a politics of "faith, family and flag", but the foundation of these beliefs rests on a deep suspicion of creative destruction because it is so disruptive to settled patterns of life and work.

David Goodhart, who has written extensively on the politics of immigration, draws a distinction between people he describes as "anywheres" and "somewheres" (Goodhart 2017). "Anywheres" are the beneficiaries of the changes in the structure of capitalism over the last 40 years. They are university educated, have high-level skills, feel comfortable wherever they happen to be in the world, are socially and economically liberal and value openness, tolerance and diversity. "Somewheres" are less well educated, more geographically rooted, hostile to immigration, culturally conservative and almost certainly voted for the UK to leave the EU. They are also more likely to endorse the statement that Britain feels like a foreign country today. Blue Labour is a politics consecrated to the interests of the "somewheres", as exemplified by Glasman's call for a halt to all immigration in 2011.

And yet, below the surface of Glasman's rhetoric is a fairly orthodox social democratic programme. There is an emphasis on the importance of craft skills as a source of occupational identity and self-respect, proposals to reform corporate governance to give workers' representatives the right to participate in decision-making, support for co-determination (works councils) on the German model to give workers real influence over what happens to them at work from one day to the next and endorsement of community-based living wage campaigns to build solidarity *and* address the deep-rooted problem of low pay. We could go so far as to say that Blue Labour is little more than conventional German social democracy in an English nationalist wrapper. Nonetheless, those who are socially liberal, comfortable with diversity and support the UK's continued membership of the EU are unlikely to be enthused by a narrow, 'Little Englander' nationalism, even if that wagon is hitched, somewhat inelegantly, to support for a social market economy.

The faith and family components of Blue Labour are equally problematic, not least because the UK is now a largely secular nation[12]. It is true that the level of faith commitment is higher in black and minority ethnic communities, but the white working class, in common with the majority of white Britons, has abandoned religious observance. The suggestion that progressive political success depends on a revival of belief in God is odd, to say the least. Furthermore, a socially conservative politics of the family can easily lead to privileging some household types and stigmatising others. 'Family values' are used by socially conservative Tories to oppose abortion, attack single parenthood and reject the case for equal marriage. For Blue Labour this is a not very well concealed elephant trap, which could fracture the progressive coalition.

George Orwell, in *The Lion and the Unicorn* and *Notes on Nationalism*, drew a distinction between patriotism, defined as a belief in and commitment to one's country, and nationalism, the conviction that one's country or race is superior to all others (Orwell 1941, Orwell 1945). Britain's defiance of the Nazis was a classic expression of patriotism, whereas the Nazis' effort to dominate Europe was the brutal expression of the politics of nationalism.

We might note too, taking Orwell's example, that victory against the Nazis was a fine example of international collaboration in the service of patriotic ends.

For much of the 1980s Labour was seen as an unpatriotic party, principally because the commitment to unilateral nuclear disarmament was viewed as a refusal to take the nation's defence seriously. One reason for the 1997 landslide was that Blair and his colleagues had made it abundantly clear that a Labour government was committed to the nuclear deterrent and Nato membership. Nobody, at that time, could have argued convincingly that Labour was unpatriotic. New Labour also understood the importance of symbols in this context – Peter Mandelson's photo opportunity with a bulldog in the 1997 general election campaign is a frivolous example. And Gordon Brown devoted considerable intellectual energy to the development of a distinctive notion of Britishness, partly to make the case against Scottish nationalism, but also to align Labour's values with British values.

None of these efforts was entirely successful and perhaps the best response to Blue Labour's endorsement of faith, family and flag is to return to Orwell's distinction. Patriotism can be inclusive, accepting of plural identities and entirely consistent with the notion that the national interest is best served by international collaboration, not least through the EU. If Glasman is right to argue that Labour can only win the support of the working class by being patriotic then Orwell's approach is most likely to enable the party to achieve that goal without losing critical elements of the electoral coalition.

When measured up against our four questions, Blue Labour accurately describes the experience of communities under pressure, offers a fairly conventional social democratic policy prospectus but then runs the risk of fracturing Labour's electoral coalition by taking the party deep into the waters of exclusivist nationalism. Moreover, Blue Labour carries a good deal of essentially conservative ideological baggage that is both inconsistent with Labour's intellectual traditions and could potentially raise expectations that cannot be met.

By placing such emphasis on continuity and custom it disavows, at least to some degree, the reality that change is a constant.

Alternatively, one might say that Blue Labour is characterised by ambiguity in its attitude to social and economic change, with an obvious tension between preserving the status quo on the one hand and managing change differently on the other. Once shorn of the nationalistic, anti-EU rhetoric, what is most striking about Blue Labour, perhaps, is the similarity to the ideas associated with the stakeholder model of capitalism promoted by thinkers on the fringes of New Labour in the middle 1990s (Hutton 1995). We have already seen, however, that the social market or co-ordinated market models of capitalism have not provided an effective defence against rightwing populism. There must be real doubt about whether making the UK a little more like Germany is sufficient to the challenges confronting working-class communities under pressure today. Restrictions on immigration in particular are unlikely to improve the opportunities of the most disadvantaged. Blue Labour's weakness, therefore, is that it is too nationalistic and insufficiently radical in responding to the realities of creative destruction.

A revived New Labour centrism?

The fourth and final lens through which party members are invited to view the world is a revival of the centrist politics associated with New Labour. Supporters of this view would argue that there is still considerable political advantage to be gained from presenting New Labour's synthesis of "traditional values in a modern setting" to the electorate once again. The combination of economic dynamism and social justice; investment in public services and the reform of delivery; tough on crime, tough on the causes of crime; action to tackle child poverty coupled with welfare reform; and, education, education, education are still resonant policies that can win majority support. In large measure, this argument is open to the same objection as the case advanced by Ken Loach in *The Spirit of '45*: there is nothing to be gained by dwelling on the glories of past achievements.

The world has moved on and the problems confronting the country today are not the problems of 1997.

Ed Miliband won the 2010 leadership contest because he offered a marginally different economic analysis to his brother, at least admitting the possibility that the Labour government had been too timorous in confronting concentrations of economic power. Moreover, Miliband also offered some measured criticism of the government's failures, suggesting that insufficient attention had been given to the reduction of income inequality, that the programme of public service reform had defaulted to a 'private good, public bad' setting, that the defence of social security had been less than robust and that too little had been done to tackle regional imbalances in prosperity, especially in medium-sized towns and cities.

The tragedy was, of course, that as leader, Miliband never developed this critique into a convincing model for reformist social democracy. By the time of the 2015 leadership contest the mainstream candidates had no comprehensive narrative that made sense of the world, leaving Corbyn as the only contender who seemed to have a set of core beliefs offering hope for the future – even if, in reality, the Corbyn agenda is simply deep-frozen Bennery, minus all the interesting ingredients, refreshed in the microwave after 30 years.

It is reasonable to conclude, therefore, that our four political questions cannot be answered simply by looking back to 1997. What can be learned from New Labour's experience, nonetheless, is the importance of having a clear understanding of social and political realities. Just as Bernstein recommended, Blair and his colleagues, at least in the early period, were seized of the need to understand the electorate's anxieties, develop a policy programme that addressed the problems of the day, offer the prospect of improvement in the future and identify a limited number of priorities. If the task in the middle 1990s was to create a left politics that offered hope while also being unthreatening, then New Labour was a superlative achievement.

THE CASE FOR REVISIONISM:
TOWARDS A NEW SYNTHESIS

A supporter of the current Labour leadership would no doubt argue that the agonising of the preceding pages is entirely unnecessary. There is no need to learn from New Labour or any other current in Labour's ideological stream. Under Corbyn the Labour party is the most popular democratic socialist party in Europe, having won 40% of the popular vote at the 2017 general election. Social democrats from continental sister parties should be beating a path to Corbyn's door, seeking his advice and assistance as they struggle to recover from a series of ignominious defeats.

There are several responses that might be given to this criticism, the most obvious of which is that, despite the awful Conservative campaign, Labour failed to win the 2017 general election. A more sophisticated reaction would draw attention to the difference between the UK's first past the post system and the proportional representation systems in continental Europe. Across the UK, or at least in England and Wales, all progressive forces gravitated to Labour because they had nowhere else to go – the Liberal Democrats had destroyed their credibility by participating in the coalition government and the Greens were never more than a marginal force. In continental Europe, on the other hand, progressive forces are divided and have found it hard to collaborate effectively to marshal anti-conservative voters behind a compelling prospectus.

One reading of the Corbyn ascendancy is that Labour, previously a social democratic party of sorts, is now a leftwing populist party, closer to Syriza in Greece or Podemos in Spain than to PASOK or the PSOE. Labour, under the Corbyn-McDonnell leadership, is best seen as a new party that has little in common with its antecedents. But even if this analysis is correct, the Corbynistas are still left with the dilemma that a purely populist manifesto is never a recipe for successful government. Tragic choices and ruthless prioritisation are unavoidable features of political life.

So how should we begin our quest for a more effective progressive politics? A useful starting point is to recognise that none of the diverse accounts offered in this chapter is completely satisfying, although they all offer useful insights into the challenges faced by the left (broadly defined). Corbynism, despite its weaknesses, shows us how a populist strategy can mobilise those previously disengaged from the political process. It also, in present circumstances, has more resonance with the electorate than more responsible or technocratic narratives. Paul Mason's technological determinism, while flawed, reminds us of the realities of creative destruction and the disruption to settled patterns of work and life. Blue Labour tells us that people need security and cultural confidence if they are to thrive in a world characterised by disruptive change. And New Labour tells us that recognising the undoubted advantages of properly regulated markets has to be the foundation on which a successful progressive politics must be built.

Each of these ideological lenses may be partial and offer a slightly distorted view of the world, but they have enough in common to constitute the basis for a conversation. What Labour and other social democratic parties need is an open discussion engaging all the legitimate strains in the ideological tradition. Of course, this rules out revolutionary Marxists, the 57 varieties of Trotskyist and probably a small number of Labour party members too. As Neil Kinnock consistently argued, even a broad church needs walls and Labour's walls, under the current leadership, have become a little too permeable.

The remainder of this volume is written in the spirit that there is no right answer just waiting to be discovered by a political genius with penetrating insight. It is equally wrong to believe that success in a general election is to be derived from a factional victory inside the party. What is offered here is tentative, provisional and open to discussion.

The only foundational principle that is non-negotiable is an acceptance of the continued existence of capitalism. Social democrats (and democratic socialists too) must, however reluctantly, agree that the pursuit of profit in a market-based system will continue to be the basis for the production of most goods and services.

Social democrats must also return to first principles in considering how the state can support people in conditions of uncertainty. The technological determinists may be wrong to believe that the machines have now taken on the role of the proletariat as the agents of social transformation, but they are right to argue that digital technologies could, in a transitional period, prove highly disruptive to settled patterns of life and work. An obvious conclusion is that unemployment insurance systems must do more than simply offer people replacement income, conditional on looking for a new job. Labour market programmes must be developed which support individuals to acquire the capabilities they need to find a secure place in the changing world of work. Activating the unemployed to look for work is obviously important, but investing in human capital is essential too. Social democrats should affirm their commitment to full employment too; decent work remains the most effective anti-poverty strategy and tight labour markets offer the best prospect that wages will rise in line with productivity. It is to the issue of work and its place in a revived politics of the left that we now turn.

LABOUR AS THE PARTY OF WORK AND WORKERS

A social democratic political economy?

Flexibility is used today as another way to lift the curse of oppression from capitalism. In attacking rigid bureaucracy and emphasising risk, it is claimed, flexibility gives people more freedom to shape their lives. In fact, the new order substitutes new controls rather than simply abolishing the rules of the past – but these rules are hard to understand. The new capitalism is often an illegible regime of power.

Richard Sennett, *The Corrosion of Character* (1998)

WORK: MISSING FROM THE LEFT'S NARRATIVE?

The focus of the discussion so far has been on the failure of the left to offer adequate guarantees of either security or opportunity to significant sections of the community, leading to a fracturing of the progressive coalition. Part of the story is about the retreat of the welfare state and the decline of institutions, like trade unions, which historically had sustained the left in tough times. But an important element, absent from the left's narrative for more than 30 years, is the place of work in the lives of citizens. This is surprising, not least because central to the promise of both democratic socialism and social democracy is a commitment to end exploitation, to ensure that workers receive a just reward for their efforts and, viewed through a Marxist lens, to end the alienation of workers from their labour.

It is especially striking, when the left was winning elections from the middle 1990s to the middle 2000s, that 'work' was rarely given serious attention as an indispensable ingredient in a modernised social democracy. Certainly, there was an emphasis on jobs and some effort was made, albeit in rather muted language, to reinstate full employment as an objective of public policy. But the notion that governments could (or should) take decisive action to shift the balance of power between capital and labour in labour's direction was well beyond the limits of any modernising consensus.

Instead, the focus was on the importance of labour market flexibility as a necessary condition of high levels of employment. One can see this in both the rhetoric and the practice of the Blair and Brown governments, in the labour market policies of the SPD under Gerhard Schröder and in the pronouncements of organisations like the OECD, the IMF and the World Bank. There was a general agreement across social democratic parties that governments should establish minimum standards to prevent exploitation, but beyond that more ambitious policies were viewed as an unwelcome intrusion. To understand the labour market policies of the 1997–2010 Labour government, all one need do is review the OECD's 1994 *Jobs Study*, which contained an extremely orthodox statement of the importance of labour market flexibility (OECD 1994).

It is worth noting, however, that the OECD, in its reassessment of the *Jobs Study* in 2004, stepped back from an unqualified endorsement of the Anglo-Saxon model of labour market flexibility (OECD 2004). In part, this was because the evidence showed more than one route to strong jobs growth. For example, in the Nordic countries and the Netherlands (to some extent), strong collective bargaining institutions, social dialogue, generous out-of-work benefits, rigorous job search requirements and investment in human capital constituted a package of policies that were just as successful at creating jobs as the deregulated Anglo-Saxon model. A judicious mix of flexibility and security seemed to have been achieved, to which the neologism 'flexicurity' was applied.

Some commentators, including the present author, suggested that Labour in government ought to have drawn some inspiration from the model developed in these countries; preserving a high degree of labour market flexibility, anticipating disruptive labour market trends, and offering workers support when their industries were affected by creative destruction. But all these initiatives, while admirable, were insufficient to offset powerful forces undermining established forms of employment and stable communities. Denmark, Sweden and the Netherlands have all witnessed a retreat from social democracy and a resurgence of the far right. If the mainstream left wants to recover lost strength then the weaknesses of *all* the pre-crisis labour market models must be recognised and a bolder prospectus adopted, offering citizens real security in conditions of change.

LABOUR'S PROBLEM

It may seem absurd to suggest that Labour could be anything other than a broad-based party representing the interests of all those who work, but there is polling and focus group evidence to suggest that the contrary may be the case. Some former Labour voters appear to believe that the party no longer represents 'people like me', embracing what might be thought of as a series of rightwing prejudices; that the party is more concerned about the interests of those who do not and do not wish to work. This could be viewed as a revolt of the "somewheres" against the "anywheres"; it certainly helps to explain the Conservative victories in formerly safe seats like Stoke-on-Trent South, Mansfield and Walsall North along with the significant reduction in the Labour vote in towns like Ashfield and Bishop Auckland. If Labour wants to win a majority in the next general election then it must halt and reverse this trend.

Of course, the fact that all these constituencies had majorities favouring Brexit is another factor that cannot be ignored. But one is driven to the conclusion that losing support in what can best be described as working-class seats endorses the Blue Labour argument that the party has experienced an erosion of its previously strong connection with a significant minority of working people who, in the past, would never have voted anything but Labour.

A useful starting point would be to affirm Labour's commitment to full and fulfilling employment, making the case that decent jobs for all are an essential ingredient in a successful modern economy. But emphasising this commitment alone will not be sufficient to win back sceptical working-class voters or those middle-class centrist voters who have deserted Labour since the early 2000s.

The *Taylor Review of Modern Employment Practices*, which reported to the Conservative government last year, made a compelling case that the issue of job quality should be a political priority for all parties. The policy recommendations were rather weak, but the argument itself is sound. What Labour needs to offer is a positive and persuasive case for "good work", remembering that "increasing the power of the worker at the point of production" is an orthodox social democratic objective.

A sceptical reader might say that this is all very well, but Labour has won healthy majorities in the past without having a comprehensive story about the place of work in the lives of citizens. Nor has Labour ever offered a distinctively social democratic vision of working life. To some extent this is true, but it reflects the division of responsibilities that used to exist between Labour and its affiliated trade unions. A Labour government's job was to maintain full employment and improve the quality and range of public services; workplace issues were the exclusive province of the trade unions[1]. This division of responsibilities was eroded over time when it became clear that trade unions could not, acting alone, address gender pay inequality, race discrimination in employment or the weak protections available to workers in non-union workplaces. That is why governments took legislative action and began to create today's framework of individual employment rights. Moreover, the current diminished status of trade unions and collective bargaining means that the industrial wing of the movement is struggling to play its historic role.

Social democrats may wish for a revival of trade unionism and collective bargaining, but that will be a long-term enterprise and there are problems that need to be addressed today. As we shall see, a commitment to industrial democracy is central to a modernised social democracy, which means that government must act to ensure that people enjoy the same rights in the workplace that they enjoy as citizens – freedom of association, freedom of speech, the right to put their case to their employer, individually and collectively, and receive a reasoned response.

A BOLD VISION OF 'GOOD WORK'

At this point it is worth dealing with another potential objection: that people have such different preferences and expectations at work that it makes no sense to talk about "good work" at all. Proponents of this view will argue that some people may be career focused, whereas for others a job is just a job; some may enjoy work that others find tedious; some may prefer working with their hands, others doing work that is intellectually demanding (see Shackleton in Coats 2009). No doubt this is true to some extent, but it is not quite the point under discussion. The case being made here is that some features of working life have an adverse impact on *everybody*, no matter what their preferences and aspirations may be. Removing these negative factors will lead to higher-quality work and better workplaces.

To begin with, it is clear that being in work is superior to worklessness. Unemployment has a corrosive effect on physical and mental health, is devastating to personal confidence and damaging to relationships (Marmot 2004, Layard 2005). It is entirely reasonable, therefore, to conclude that getting the unemployed or inactive back into work and keeping them there must be a priority for all governments.

It can also be said with certainty that "bad work" has a damaging effect on both health and life expectancy (Marmot 2004). This is not simply a matter of exposure to back-breaking physical labour, hazardous substances or technologies. What are generally considered to be good jobs can also be viewed as bad work. The following features of the workplace are associated with a range of medical conditions:

- Insecure employment.
- A lack of control or autonomy over the organisation of work.
- An imbalance between the effort workers make and the rewards that they receive. In part this is about pay, but a lack of recognition or respect for tasks performed well can also have an adverse effect.
- Unfair treatment and in particular a lack of procedural justice (Kivimaki 2007).
- Poor workplace relationships, both with managers and with colleagues.
- An absence of voice or influence over critical management decisions.

One can see, therefore, how a 'good job', as conventionally conceived, can deliver bad work. Office cleaners, security guards, a worker in a Sports Direct warehouse, investment bankers and corporate lawyers can all experience a loss of autonomy and control, poor workplace relationships, bullying, harassment, unfair treatment and an imbalance between effort and reward. 'Good work for all' can be a unifying argument, building on shared experience and used to make the case that, at the very least, government should regulate to fix the background conditions shaping contractual relationships.

A sceptical reader may say that the argument is interesting and, at the level of policy, offers some useful guidance for progressive politicians. But 'more autonomy at work' is not the most compelling slogan. Social democrats need a more expansive and popular statement of how the world of work should be reshaped to achieve progressive objectives. Furthermore, developing a compelling proposition is not just a matter of convincing workers that their experience can and should be better; employers have to be part of this equation too and need to understand that offering decent conditions for all is essential for organisational success.

Another way to describe the good workplace is to say that high-quality employment relationships rest on respect for three principles: efficiency, equity and voice (Budd 2004). *Efficiency* matters because all organisations, whether in the public or private sector, must be successful if they are to have a long-term future. *Equity* matters for all the reasons we have described: perceived unfairness in management style or culture, pay or reward all have adverse effects on both individuals and organisations. *Voice,* is nothing more than a recognition that the principles we value in democratic societies are just as relevant once a worker has crossed their employer's threshold. Industrial democracy must be reinstated as a central commitment of modern social democracy.

The next step in the argument must be to review the realities of work today. This matters for both policy, because social democrats need to know what problems they are trying to solve, and for political narrative, because Labour needs a story that resonates with work as it is experienced by the majority of citizens. It is to those issues that we now turn.

LABOUR MARKET REALITIES

Persistence or change?

Much of the popular commentary about recent labour market developments has focused on the rise of the zero hours contract (ZHC) and the problems experienced by workers in the gig economy. It would be absurd to deny that there is a problem of exploitation associated with these forms of work but it would be equally wrong to conclude that a wave of casualisation is sweeping away permanent employee jobs. The official labour market statistics suggest, for example, that there has been as much persistence as change over the last 30 years on the dimensions of contractual status (Figure 3.1). Employees with permanent contracts still account for almost four in every five people at work. The extent of temporary work fluctuates with the economic cycle, but has remained relatively stable, rising no higher than 6% of total employment. Moreover, despite the widespread belief that more workers are having to take second jobs to make ends meet, fewer than 4% of people report that they are in this position. There is little evidence here of a labour market transformed.

The same might be said for much of the recent concern about the supposed boom in self-employment, often seen as a consequence of the rise of the gig economy. In 1986 around one in 10 people at work were self-employed. In 2017 the figure was closer to one in seven. There is no doubt that self-employment has risen since the global financial crisis, which in part may be explained as making a virtue of necessity – having lost their permanent employee job and armed with a redundancy payment workers decide to strike out on their own. Whatever the reason for these recent trends, a 3% rise in self-employment over a 30-year period hardly constitutes a 'boom'.

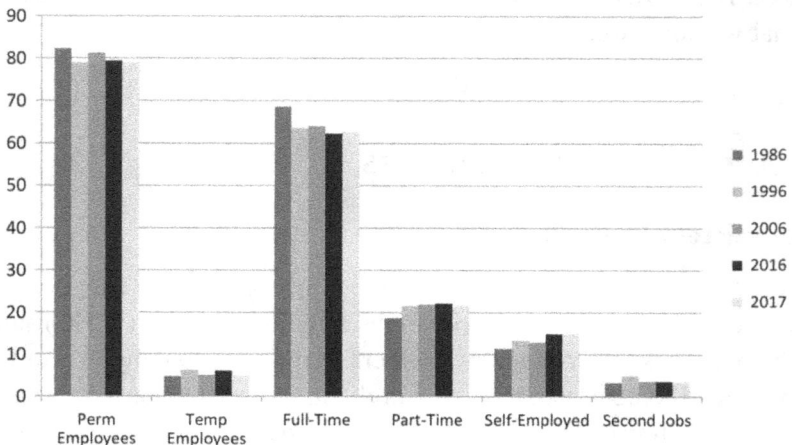

Figure 3.1   The labour market and contractual status (% of all in employment). *Source:* ONS.

What do we know about the gig economy?

Rather extravagant claims have also been made about the supposedly inexorable rise of the gig economy, where people are misclassified as self-employed, required to undertake particular tasks rather than accept a contract of employment and are therefore denied rights to sick pay, holiday pay or the national minimum wage. A recent study included a headline figure that there are now 5 million crowd workers in the UK, with 9 million people reporting that they have tried to find work through digital platforms like Uber, Upwork, Handy and TaskRabbit (Huws et al. 2016).[2] These figures are undeniably striking, but a moment's reflection suggests that they may not be entirely credible. If the official figures for permanent employment are correct (there is no reason to cast doubt on them), it seems surprising, to say the least, that almost one in three people are trying to find work through a digital platform. What the more detailed analysis of the crowd working study also shows, however, is that only one in ten of those responding found *any* work through an app and only 1 in 20 derived all their income from these arrangements. Even that figure looks somewhat excessive when compared with research in the US, which suggests that between 0.4% and 0.5% of the workforce are finding employment through digital platforms (Harris and Krueger 2015, Katz and Krueger 2016).

It is also worth noting that most of the increase in self-employment in the UK since 2010 can be found in the top three occupational groups (managers, professionals and associate professionals) (Brinkley 2016). This also helps to explain the flurry of policy interest in the growth of 'freelancing' which, for these purposes, is defined as own-account self-employment in those top three groups. According to the most recent study around 6% of all those in employment were working as freelancers in 2015 (Kitching 2016). There is also a high level of churn in this population, with almost one in three entering and exiting the freelance workforce every year.

If we are really in search of the gig economy then this is where it is most likely to be found: amongst those working as professionals in, for example, the creative industries, engineering/construction and management consulting. It is self-evident that this group is not low paid, although they may be uncertain about the precise projects on which they may be working in six months' time. Life is characterised by a degree of uncertainty and potentially a high level of income insecurity (if contracts dry up). Skilled, professional people are, however, unlikely to be out of the labour market and without work for long.

Arguably, the debate about the realities of the gig economy has been distorted by the degree of attention given to two companies: Uber and Deliveroo. In both of those cases the employer has claimed that they are not an employer at all, but a digital platform through which people can secure a degree of flexibility, working on particular tasks (driving a cab, delivering food) at times of their choosing. Arguably, this is nothing more than an abuse of market power. Both companies claim that those using the platform are self-employed entrepreneurs but, as a recent employment tribunal decision made clear, this is a poor description of the realities of the relationship. Those driving cabs using the Uber app were found by the tribunal to be workers (an intermediate legal status between employed and self-employed) and therefore entitled to the national minimum wage and paid holidays. It was quite wrong to believe, as Uber suggested, that the drivers were running businesses on their own account.

What these two cases prove is that the flexibility of the UK's labour market works, all too often, in the interests of the unscrupulous or those who seek to avoid their responsibilities as employers. The problem is not so much a consequence of new forms of employment but of inequalities of power that offer advantages to corporations rather than workers. The problem is not new and has existed in various forms in the construction industry for a prolonged period.

Zero-hours contracts

The account given so far has suggested that there is a big difference between the real extent of labour market change and the popular media narrative about the world of work. There is no boom in self-employment and those workers most open to exploitation in the gig economy are not really working in the gig economy at all. It is all too easy for anecdotes to be extrapolated as trends and for rare but egregious cases to be presented as if they are widespread experiences. Three years ago, long before anybody was talking about Uber or Deliveroo, the focus was on the problems experienced by workers with zero-hours contracts (ZHCs). In that case too there was a sense that most new jobs were being created in this low-quality category, decent work was disappearing and an unavoidable result was discontent and anger, fuelling the rise of populism.

Unfortunately, this narrative is mostly false. Again, there can be no doubt that the number of people with ZHCs has risen in recent years. Initially, the official statistics found it hard to capture the realities, reporting what appeared to be a rapid acceleration in the growth of the phenomenon. Arguably, some of this increase could be accounted for by the increased publicity given to zero-hours arrangements, which led to more people reporting that they were working under a ZHC, even though they had always worked under a contract of this kind. Moreover, despite the rapid increase in the recording of ZHCs, the numbers affected remain relatively small. According to the most recent data, 883,000 people reported they had a zero-hours contract in the period April–June 2017 – three in every hundred people at work. This figure is dwarfed by the one in five, or 6.4 million workers, in the UK who count as low paid on the internationally recognised definition – they have earnings below two-thirds of the median.

It is important to understand too that not everybody with a ZHC is either low paid or exploited. Agency nurses in the NHS, for example, will count as ZHC workers because they have no fixed hours of work. Furthermore, according to the TUC's research, around half of all ZHC workers were low paid in 2016[3] (TUC 2017). This suggests that the number of ZHC workers falling into the vulnerable category is 441,000 or 1.4% of all people at work.[4] It is certainly true that these workers are having an exceptionally difficult time both in making ends meet and in matching their working patterns to their domestic responsibilities. But it is quite wrong to say that the problems experienced either by those with ZHCs or by the bogus self-employed in the gig economy are especially widespread. If Labour wants to tell a compelling and generally appealing story about the changing world of work then it needs to look elsewhere for inspiration.

Insecurity in the mainstream: The job quality problem

A better point of departure than the focus on the worst cases of exploitation is a recognition that a significant minority (and in some cases a majority) of people in apparently secure, mainstream employment find work a troublesome experience too. The *Workplace Employment Relations Study* (WERS) reports that there was a significant increase in the intensity of work between 2004–2011, with more than four in every five employees (83%) reporting that "my job requires me to work very hard" (van Wanrooy et al. 2013). That finding is confirmed by the 2012 *Skills and Employment Survey*, which recorded that the intensity of work had remained stable in the early to middle 2000s following a significant increase in the 1990s but that work intensification gathered pace after the global crisis (Felstead et al. 2013). Moreover, almost one in four workers (23%) reported that they had to work at very high speeds most of the time.

Other important findings from the *Skills and Employment Survey* include:

- A third of employees (31%) reported that they were concerned about unfair treatment at work.
- Just over half of all employees (52%) reported anxiety over a loss of job status (less job influence, being moved to a less skilled job, being required to move to a lower-paid job, being moved to a less interesting job) (Gallie et al. 2013).
- Job-related wellbeing, when measured on the dimensions of enthusiasm for the job and contentment with the job, fell significantly from 2006 to 2012. This is largely attributed to the rise in

the percentage of people reporting high job stress (almost one in five employees (17%).
- Three in every four employees (73%) reported that they had limited influence over the organisation of their work.
- Just over one in three workers (34%) reported that they had received more than 10 days' training in the previous year – a fall from 38% in 2006.

That all is not well was explored in more detail in the *British Workplace Behaviour Survey* (Fevre 2012). This sought to identify the extent of unfair treatment across the labour market. It was inspired by the rising level of concern with bullying in the workplace but adopted a more sophisticated approach, examining unreasonable treatment, incivility, disrespect and violence. Not surprisingly, workplace violence was relatively rare, but the other phenomena were very widespread indeed. Unreasonable treatment included such experiences as having one's views and opinions ignored or being given an unreasonable workload. Incivility and disrespect included rudeness, persistent criticism and feeling threatened in the workplace (but not the threat of physical violence). Unreasonable treatment was reported by most workers as more of a concern than incivility or disrespect. The most important findings are as follows:

- Half the British workforce (52%) had experienced some form of unreasonable treatment in the two years before the survey was conducted.
- Nearly one in four workers experienced three or more different kinds of unreasonable treatment and one in 10 workers had to put up with five or more kinds of unreasonable treatment.
- Two in every five workers (40%) had been subjected to incivility and disrespect in the two years before the survey was conducted.
- One in three workers had been given an unreasonable workload.
- One in five workers were employed in a "troubled workplace" where the experience of unfair treatment (on all dimensions) was persistent rather than intermittent.

What is most striking about these experiences is that they are more prevalent amongst people in the labour market mainstream, including those with management responsibilities. The "troubled workplaces" are not simply those usually considered as offering low-quality jobs and include household name brands, generally considered to offer decent work at reasonable rates of pay. Once again, it seems that apparently 'good jobs' can deliver 'bad work'. The clear implication of this research is that some organisations incentivise managers to behave unreasonably because unreasonable behaviour is seen as a reasonable price to pay for meeting targets, implementing a restructuring programme or achieving some change in workers' behaviour.

Most importantly, perhaps, the evidence strongly suggests that the UK struggles to respect the principles of industrial citizenship. A majority of workers have no effective mechanisms, whether individual or collective, through which they can articulate their concerns to their employer. The practice of joint consultation, which used to be so widespread, is now a minority pursuit. Less than one in 10 workplaces had any joint consultation arrangements in place in 2011 and the numbers will be lower today. Almost two thirds of employees were dissatisfied with their level of involvement in workplace decision-making. Half of all employees believed that managers could not be trusted to keep their promises (van Wanrooy 2013).

At this point, perhaps, we should remind ourselves that the biggest change in the UK labour market in the last 30 years has been the decline of trade union membership and collective bargaining coverage (Figure 3.2). In 1979 almost half the workforce were union members and almost four in every five people at work had their pay and conditions determined by collective bargaining. Today, less than a quarter of employees are trade union members and around the same percentage have their pay determined by a collective agreement. The idea that workers might have a conversation with the employer about the fairness of rewards has been abandoned in most private sector workplaces.

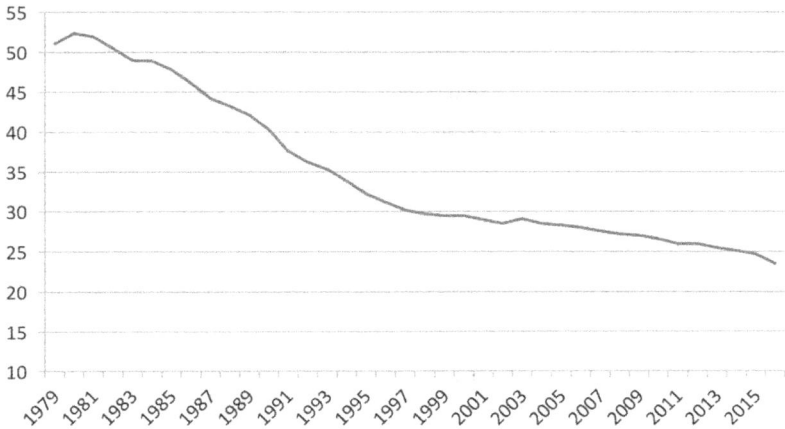

Figure 3.2 Trade union membership density 1979–2016 (% all employees). *Source:* ONS, union membership statistics.

It is not too fanciful to suggest, therefore, that many British workplaces have embraced a new feudalism, where employers are able to behave with baronial authority and workers have to do as they are told. Far from being participants or active citizens, most workers surrender Rawls' basic liberties at the point they cross their employer's threshold.

Wage stagnation

Much has been made of the absence of significant wage growth in the period since the global financial crisis. Living standards have been stagnant for far too many working households. The essential proposition can be summarised as follows: in the nine years following 2008, per capita incomes grew by 2% in total. Wages took nine years to grow as much as they would have in one 'normal' year before the crisis. Some of the phenomenon might be attributed to structural weaknesses, particularly the UK's poor productivity performance. But much of what has happened is explained by the changing balance of power between workers and their employers.

In a world where trade unions are disempowered or absent it is very difficult for workers to secure their fair share of the fruits of growth.

Recent forecasts suggest that the situation will get worse in the immediate future. According to the Resolution Foundation, while there was some modest recovery in living standards in 2015–2016, data from the Office of Budgetary Responsibility (OBR) projects consistent reductions in household disposable incomes over 19 successive quarters to 2020. Incomes in the top half of the distribution are expected to rise modestly, median income will continue to stagnate and those in the bottom half of the distribution will experience a significant fall in incomes (Corlett et al. 2017).

We have already seen, in Chapter 1, that the UK had a wages problem before the crisis (Commission on Living Standards 2012). Deliberate and reasonably transparent policy decisions have brought the world to the current conjuncture. It was no secret that Margaret Thatcher and Ronald Reagan were hostile to unions and supportive of deregulation; nor was it a secret that Germany's Red-Green coalition, led by Gerhard Schröder, wanted to create more low wage employment to 'solve' Germany's unemployment problem.[5] There is no rigging or conspiracy at work here. Electorates voted for these policies, even though they may not have been fully aware of the consequences.

It would be wrong to attribute the rise of populism *entirely* to changes in labour market policy, but it would be equally wrong to say that public policy is of no importance whatsoever. A foundational assumption in the world of work is that workers can expect to share in the fruits of growth generated by their employer's business. There is an expectation of fairness and a belief that hard work will be rewarded. The disconnection of pay growth from productivity growth undermines all of these assumptions. Returning to our earlier discussion, it erodes the ontological security on which the social order depends. Solid ground has become quicksand. Certainty is replaced by insecurity and the social contract is broken. Dealing with these anxieties must be just as much of a priority as dealing with the difficulties experienced by workers at the margins of the labour market.

The persistence of low pay

It has already been recorded that while workers with ZHCs have a very high risk of being low paid, the numbers constitute a small proportion – around 7% – of the low paid working population. The UK is unusual in having a relatively high percentage of low paid workers and in the persistence of the problem. In 2016 around 6.4 million workers, or almost one in five people at work were low paid according to the accepted international definition – two thirds of median earnings (Figure 3.3).

Some readers may find this surprising, believing that the introduction of the national minimum wage ought to have eliminated low pay from the UK economy. There can be no doubt that the national minimum wage has had an impact in eliminating extreme low pay – nobody in Britain is now working for less than half the median – but the problems of living on a low income remain. Households struggle to make ends meet and recent forecasts point to the probability of downward pressure on incomes for all those in the bottom half of the distribution (Corlett et al. 2017).

The present government's strategy to reduce low pay remains that developed by the former chancellor George Osborne; the Low

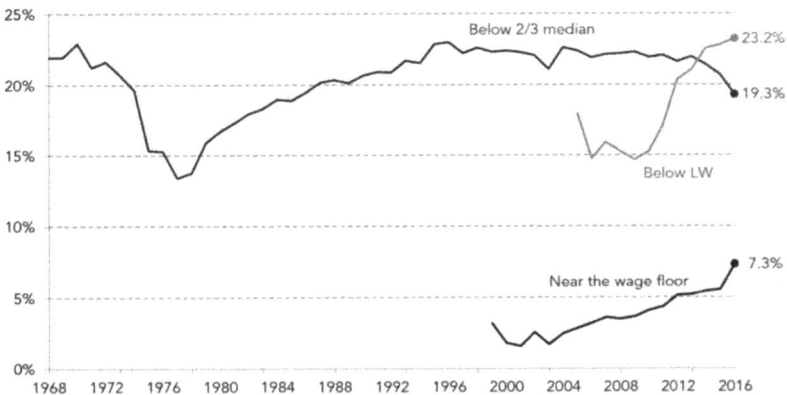

Figure 3.3 Percentage of workers below selected low pay thresholds 1968–2016. *Source:* Resolution Foundation.

Pay Commission (LPC) has essentially been instructed to deliver increases in the national minimum wage to ensure the level reaches 60% of median earnings by 2020. Whether this target remains achievable in a post-Brexit world must be an open question, not least because employers may have legitimate complaints about large increases in the national minimum wage when their businesses are under pressure. Paradoxically, the Conservative government's support for a higher national minimum wage may have the effect of reducing employer support for the measure. The independence of the LPC has also been undermined by direct political intervention in the determination of the appropriate level.

As the Resolution Foundation noted, the projected rises in the national minimum wage for those over the age of 25 have not reduced the percentage of workers below the 'real' living wage – the income level fixed by the Living Wage Foundation which is supposed to lift people out of working poverty and allow for full social participation (D'Arcy 2017). There are already some indications that the consequence of the government's strategy for the reduction of low pay is a bunching of earnings just *above* the level of the national minimum wage. Statistically, as the national minimum approaches 60% of the median, the percentage of workers defined as low paid must fall. But if they are earning something close to the low pay threshold or the wage floor it is legitimate to ask whether this has genuinely transformed their prospects. If social democrats are really concerned about expanding the practical realm of freedom for the most disadvantaged citizens then small movements in wage levels are not an adequate measure. We should return to the questions about capabilities discussed in Chapter 2: just what more can households do with marginal improvements in their incomes? If the practical difference is small and if people are still struggling to make ends meet then a more ambitious prospectus is required.

The robots are coming to take your job – or not?

We had reason in Chapter 2 to explore the argument that technology will engineer an economic revolution leading to the end of capitalism. Another interpretation of the same case is that all the concerns described in the preceding paragraphs about job quality and low pay will prove to be irrelevant once we are confronted by the irresistible march of the machines. Widespread technological unemployment is said to be in prospect.

This line of argument has a venerable pedigree, with a concern that the machines are about to take over emerging at around the same time as what we now call capitalism. Indeed, a swift glance at the history of the twentieth century confirms that every decade witnessed some commentary about the threat to employment from automation (Brinkley 2016).

Franklin Roosevelt was concerned that the New Deal would prove ineffective as automation produced an equal and opposite reaction to the government's efforts to create jobs. Keynes also believed that the necessity to work would reduce as automation progressed, with nobody needing to spend more than 15 hours a week at their workplace by the end of the twentieth century. In 1964, a report was sent to President Lyndon Johnson, which concluded that the advance of "cybernation" would soon result in an economy where:

Potentially unlimited output can be achieved by systems of machines which will require little co-operation from human beings (Ford 2015).

The eminent panel that produced the report went on to forecast massive technological unemployment and recommended a UBI as the best policy solution.

By the early 1980s, the British trade unionists Clive Jenkins and Barry Sherman had produced two volumes in a similar vein – *The Collapse of Work* (1979) and *Leisure Shock* (1981). At least Jenkins and Sherman could point to rising unemployment at the time of publication, but that was almost certainly caused by global economic conditions (the second oil price shock) and the economic policy mistakes of the early Thatcher period. In 1995 Jeremy Rifkin produced *The End of Work*, which offered another apocalyptic vision of a world without jobs – and foresaw the dawn of a "post-market era" (Rifkin 1995). Attentive readers of Paul Mason's work will recognise both the style and the over-confident predictions about the end of capitalism.

Nonetheless, those of us with a more sceptical cast of mind ought to pay attention to these predictions, not least because, in the current environment, a narrative that offers a comprehensive explanation of events has considerable political purchase. The Labour front bench claim to be interested in the UBI, it is being strongly promoted by the Royal Society of Arts (Painter and Thoung 2015) and these ideas are becoming part of the common sense of the Momentum left.

Four immediate responses might be given to the re-emergence of pessimistic technological determinism. First, capitalism has never worked this way since it emerged as an economic system in the late eighteenth century. Certainly there has been significant disruption and the challenge this poses to policymakers has been a consistent theme of this volume. But mass unemployment, when it has arisen, has been the result of policy mistakes, the retreat of the regulatory state (with governments failing to set the stage) and the irrational exuberance that characterises financial markets in particular – you can never have too much of a good thing until the bubble bursts.

Second, much of the commentary fails to distinguish between the predictions of a world without work, sometimes translated into popular parlance on the left as "fully automated luxury communism", and the undeniable reality that technological change, even though it may be beneficial in the long run, can be hugely disruptive to settled patterns of employment. The policy focus should therefore be on the likely scale of the disruption and the provision of proper support to losers from the process, not on utopian visions of a workless world where we can, following Marx, "hunt in the morning, fish in the afternoon, rear cattle in the evening".

Third, it is very hard to detect *any* sign today that unemployment can be attributed to automation. The UK's recent jobs performance is impressive – even with the caveats entered earlier about the quality of work and the persistence of low pay. There are now more people at work than at any time in the past and the employment rate (the percentage of the adult population in work) has reached an historic high of 75%. If the robots are coming for your job then they certainly are not coming tomorrow.

Fourth, it is, arguably, a major political mistake for the left to develop a narrative that depends on an inevitable digital apocalypse. Social democrats are most successful when they can offer the electorate a practical message of hope, where an incisive analysis of present discontents is related directly to a workable policy agenda. The chattering classes may have developed an obsession with technology in the years since the crisis, but most voters are likely to be motivated by more conventional concerns – health, education, wages, housing and transport. It seems absurd to argue that the fear of the robots is a factor in either the rise of Donald Trump, the resurgence of the far right across Europe or the UK's narrow majority for Brexit.

Nonetheless, even reputable analysts have fallen prey to the temptation of making eye-catching claims that are then misinterpreted in the public conversation. The principle of modesty seems very hard to observe. Perhaps the most notorious assessment is that produced by Carl Frey and Michael Osborne of the Oxford Martin School in 2013, which predicted that up to 47% of American occupations could be automated by the early 2030s. Although their evaluation was careful not to argue for high levels of technological unemployment, it was interpreted as meaning that almost half of all jobs could disappear in the near future. Of course, this is not what Frey and Osborne argued, resting their case instead on the belief that labour would be reallocated from jobs that could be performed most efficiently by machines to jobs that could only be undertaken by humans. Their central policy recommendation will be familiar to anyone who has taken an interest in public policy in recent times – develop human capital:

> Our findings thus imply that as technology races ahead, low skill workers will reallocate to tasks that are non-susceptible to computerisation ie tasks requiring creative or social intelligence. For workers to win the race, however, they will need to acquire creative or social skills (Frey and Osborne 2013).

Even with these limitations, the claim still looks a little exotic and it has been subjected to a rigorous critique by analysts at the OECD (Arntz et al. 2016). In their view, Frey and Osborne fail to distinguish between the automation of *occupations* and the automation of *tasks*, when it is the latter that has characterised most technological change in the past.

Moreover, Frey and Osborne assume that all jobs that *can* be automated *will* be automated, whereas in reality, of course, substituting capital (an intelligent machine) for labour depends on the relative cost of each factor of production and whether such an investment will produce business benefits. The widespread availability of cheap labour can easily act as a disincentive to automation.

The existing structure of a country's economy can also affect the extent of the risk to jobs from automation. So far as the UK is concerned, for example, the OECD suggest that only 10% of jobs are in the high-risk category. No country has more than 12% of jobs at high risk and for countries like South Korea and Japan no more than 7% of jobs are at high risk. Of course, this still means that more than 3 million workers in the UK could be on the receiving end of bad news from a robot. Nonetheless, this is a good deal less threatening than an analysis suggesting that some 15 million jobs could be affected. When viewed in an historical perspective the change is obviously disruptive but should be manageable.

It would be very unwise to conclude, therefore, that the welfare state needs to be fundamentally reconstructed for the transformations of the digital age. There is no need to embark on such radical departures as the UBI or plan for a fully automated world without work. For the time being, tomorrow and the day after will look very much like today. It is essential, however, to be clear about the risks, to understand that already disadvantaged communities may be the worst affected in the future and take action to ensure that those who are already left behind do not become completely disconnected from the caravan.

Our story so far confirms that the UK has a relatively poor record of responding effectively to creative destruction. While there may be time to prepare there is no cause for complacency. Even if some of the wilder forecasts are rejected, bold new initiatives are needed in industrial, regional and labour market policies, with a weak or half-hearted response adding more fuel to the populist fire.

That said, the biggest sources of disruption to settled patterns of work and life are not related to technology at all. Dealing with the consequences of climate change and ensuring that the UK meets its treaty obligations to reduce carbon emissions will require some radical departures in transport and energy policy, big changes in manufacturing processes, the retrofitting of most of the UK's housing stock and some serious rethinking of the organisation of work and the design of jobs.

Most obviously, perhaps, the biggest threat to stable job growth today is a matter of political choice. Leaving the EU without any agreement on the future relationship between the UK and the EU27 could have catastrophic consequences for labour market perfor-mance. The government's leaked impact assessment is explicit on this point: the most disadvantaged communities, those most support-ive of Brexit, will experience the biggest negative effects.

SO WHY ARE PEOPLE ANGRY?

So far this discussion has focused on the UK and it is easy to under-stand why people at work in Britain might believe that the social contract has been broken. Unfair treatment is widespread and affects those in mainstream employment just as much as those at the mar-gins. Low pay remains at a very high level and even a rising national minimum wage has not significantly shifted the percentage of the workforce below the internationally recognised low pay threshold. Wage growth for all those at the median and below is disconnected from productivity growth – and wages since the crisis have been stagnant.

Short-termism in capital markets also helps to explain some of the discontent. Directors who are focused on maximising shareholder value in the next quarter (or the next 12 months) find it hard to make the long-term commitments to workers on which the postwar settlement rested (Foroohar 2016, Kay 2003). Financial engineering becomes more important than real engineering and major corporations are seen as portfolios of assets to be managed rather than organisations with histories, distinctive cultures and particular specialisms or capabilities. It is reasonable to conclude, therefore, that the demand for short-term performance from investors is driving some of the workplace phenomena described in the preceding sections. One can see how value extraction is related to the stagnation of wages, work intensification, declining autonomy and control, the more widespread use of intrusive performance management systems and bad management practice.

The sociologist Richard Sennett, reviewing the scene in the late 1990s, suggested that the flexibility demanded by the new capitalism was having an adverse effect on "character" (Sennett 1998). Workers (and not just the 'left behind') could find no solid ground on which to stand. Workers were not running the risk of immediate job loss, but they were in a position where they could make no assumptions about their long-term futures at work, creating a growing sense of uncertainty in other spheres of life. At the time, Sennett sounded like a voice in the wilderness. Since the crisis, however, these arguments have become more widely accepted in mainstream debate and they are wholly consistent with the research findings discussed above. It is hardly surprising that there is a good deal of fear abroad in the workplace, that people believe their job status is under threat and that reported job stress is rising. In more demotic language, the evidence suggests that the middle classes can have a rotten time at work too.

Continental European readers might take comfort from the fact that their countries are not as severely afflicted by these apparently Anglo-Saxon problems; there is less low pay, trade unions are stronger, workers have guaranteed rights to be informed and consulted about workplace change and capital markets are not quite so infected with short-termism. Yet while all these statements may be true, many western European countries have still witnessed populist revolts and declining support for mainstream social democratic parties. In large measure this is simply another way of describing the observation that *all* varieties of capitalism have failed, in different degrees, to offer the security demanded by citizens.

In some countries, with France as a case in point, this may be a matter of high unemployment depriving many people of the opportunity to make progress in their lives. They just cannot find a job. In other countries much of the discontent may be attributable to the growth of income inequality over the last 30 years (Figure 3.4). What seems to matter most here are *relative* changes in the income distribution. The Nordic countries, for example, remain amongst the most egalitarian in the world, but they have all witnessed rises in inequality, with a particularly substantial increase in Sweden. All that working-class Danes or Swedes can see is that they are doing worse than their more affluent fellow citizens. The stable path through life that they believed was guaranteed is either at risk or no longer available at all. 'One rule for them, another rule for us' is

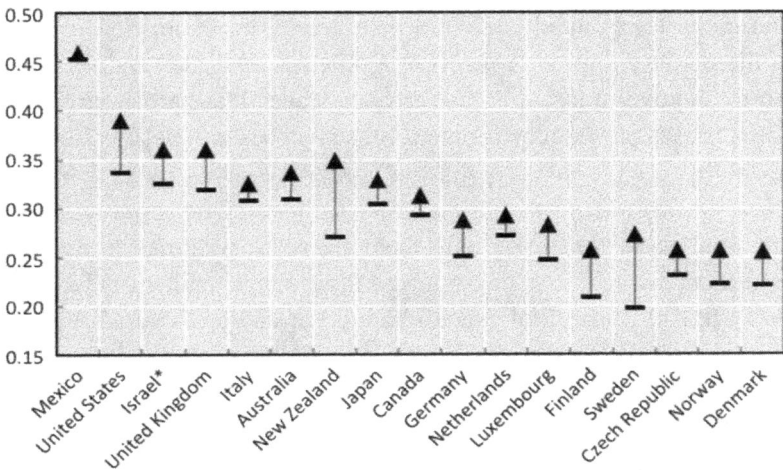

Figure 3.4 OECD countries with rising income inequality 1985–2014 (Gini coefficient). *Source:* OECD Stat.

an inevitable response to the social fractures caused by inequality, creating fertile ground for unscrupulous populists.

It would also be a mistake to believe that either the Nordic model or the German social market has offered workers a *qualitatively* different experience of industrial restructuring. Declining industrial communities look remarkably similar wherever they happen to be found in the developed world. Parts of northern England bear a strong resemblance to parts of northern France or deindustrialised parts of Germany – with the eastern Länder as an especially striking example of the phenomenon. Workers and their representatives may have been more involved in the process of restructuring in continental Europe than in either the UK or the US, but in all cases the psychological experience is one of loss; a source of secure employment has gone and is never coming back. Unless real opportunities for new jobs at similar levels of pay are available, with major public investment to provide the necessary stimulus for growth, then these communities are always going to respond to restructuring with at best grudging acquiescence and at worst open hostility.

Perhaps the best way to characterise the current situation is as follows: people can see themselves falling back; the security they had taken for granted is no longer available to them; new arrivals in the country appear to receive significant attention (and services) from the government. In these circumstances it is hardly surprising that communities under pressure ask why they are neglected when people who have just crossed the border are given more consideration. Or, in crude terms: 'it's all very well worrying about migrants, but what about me?' No doubt there are some genuine racists in all countries, but it would be wrong to think that populism is fed by a rising tide of racial intolerance – in fact the chain of causation probably works in the opposite direction, with rising racial intolerance being fed by populist discontents.

It would be equally wrong, therefore, to attribute the problems confronting the SPD in Germany to the decision by the Grand Coalition to admit 1 million refugees fleeing war and persecution. German social democracy was in some trouble long before that decision was taken. The same might be said for the Dutch Labour party, which witnessed its worst result in a generation at the most recent general election, following a decade or more of decline. And the same is true for the French socialists, who were swept from the board by hostility to Marine Le Pen amongst mainstream voters and by the success of Emmanuel Macron's *En Marche!*

A significant minority of citizens have seen their relative position deteriorate at the same time as the most affluent have seen their incomes grow significantly. The aftermath of the global crisis has crystallised these discontents, which are genuine and need to be addressed. A policy devoted entirely to controlling immigration as the only route to social democratic revival is certain to prove a blind alley.

A more sophisticated agenda, consistent with the values described in Chapter 2, must be the focus of the left's effort. Most importantly, perhaps, social democrats have to tackle the root causes and avoid being deflected by what can only be described (following Gramsci) as morbid symptoms.

AN OUTLINE POLICY AGENDA

The importance of institutions

Before we consider an outline policy agenda, there is a preliminary point that must be considered: progressive policies are most likely to endure if they are embedded in institutions that enjoy widespread support. That is the lesson of the 1945-51 governments, which built the NHS and the social security system. It can be seen in the record of the 1964–1970 and 1974–1979 governments with the establishment of the polytechnics, the creation of the Open University, the Health and Safety Commission, ACAS and the equalities commissions, now brought together under the single umbrella of the Equality and Human Rights Commission. The same is true for the Blair government, with the creation of the Low Pay Commission, the establishment of the Scottish parliament and the national assembly for Wales and the first steps towards the introduction of executive mayors in England's city-regions. Since these bodies were created they have proved very difficult to dislodge, whatever the preferences or prejudices of Conservative governments may have been. Ensuring that progressive policies are institutionally embedded is the best guarantee of continued success.

Short-termism, corporate governance and worker participation

A consistent theme of our discussion so far has been the UK's problem of short-termism in capital markets. The incentives for the inhabitants of the UK's boardrooms are equally short-term, with senior management rewards still being tied to the maximisation of shareholder value. This leads in turn to short-termism in employment relationships, not defined in terms of precarious work and temporary contracts, but in declining job quality for those with permanent, apparently secure employment, leading to what Sennett describes as the "corrosion of character" and Giddens describes as "ontological insecurity".

Any effort at reform must start with capital markets, which is why George Cox, in his report for Ed Miliband, focused on taxing the capital gains of speculative investors at higher rates than those applicable to patient capitalists who held their shares for a much longer period. Another of Cox's proposals would have given financial advantages to those who held shares for a longer period – higher dividends or access to preferential share issues – and, although he rejected the idea for immediate implementation, some consideration was given to the possibility that only those holding shares for more than a year should be able to participate in the governance of the company. The current Labour leadership would be well advised to return to some of these ideas if they are serious about changing corporate culture in the UK.

Similar arguments might be made to advance the case for worker participation in the boardroom. If a corporation is conceived as an asset owned by its shareholders with the simple mission to maximise value for those investors then a UK-style unitary board, with a mix of executive and non-executive directors, looks to be the only sensible model. If, on the other hand, a corporation is viewed as a series of communities of interest – workers, managers and investors – which owes responsibilities to each of these groups and the wider community then a rather different board structure is required. The German model of two-tier boards (a supervisory board and an executive board) is intended to strike a balance between executive decision-making and independent oversight. Workers only sit on the supervisory board. There is much that the UK could learn from this system.[6]

The case for action is compelling, which is why the *Taylor Review of Modern Employment Practices* proposed that the voice rights available to British workers should be strengthened. In response, the Conservative government has done no more than institute a review, the substance of which will focus on the threshold for triggering these rights – currently 10% of the workforce must express their support for representative consultation.

It is paradoxical, to say the least, that British workers today have more formal rights to be involved in their employers' decision-making processes than at any time in the past and fewer practical opportunities to exercise these rights. Almost all of these provisions are derived from EU directives and have been implemented *sotto voce* by successive governments, with a combination of embarrassment and a distinct lack of enthusiasm. Employers and workers have a limited awareness of these rights, if they are known at all. It would be a major advance for a Labour government to create a coherent body of law, establishing some basic rules of industrial citizenship that all enterprises must respect. More specifically, workers' representatives should have the following rights to be informed and consulted about:

- The employer's strategic plans for the business (information only).
- The likely trajectory of staffing levels in the medium term, including any threats to employment and remedial action to be taken (information and consultation).
- Significant changes to work organisation or contractual relations (I&C with a view to reaching an agreement).
- Joint management of health and safety in the workplace.
- Vocational training policies and workplace learning (I&C with a view to reaching an agreement).
- Consultation on redundancies (with a view to reaching an agreement).
- Consultation on business transfers (changes of ownership covered by the EU's Transfers of Undertakings directive) (with a view to reaching an agreement).
- Consultation on changes to occupational pensions (with a view to reaching an agreement).
- The flexible implementation of the UK's Working Time Regulations 2004 – flexibilities around the length of the working week, breaks, rest periods (with a view to reaching an agreement).

The British scholars Mark Hall and John Purcell, in their examination of the implementation of the information and consultation regulations in the UK, reviewed the experience elsewhere in the EU and concluded that the strongest predictor of de facto, practical participation is the level of mandatory worker participation prescribed by law (Hall and Purcell 2012). Public policy can create the context in which strong institutions can grow.

Low pay and wage stagnation

The Conservative government and Jeremy Corbyn's Labour party have both taken the view that significant increases in the national minimum wage are the best instrument to eliminate low pay from the UK economy. Both parties believe that significant increases in the level should be implemented with, on the Conservative model, much higher wages for those over 25 and, for Labour, much higher wages for all those over the age of 18. The flaws in this approach have already been described. It has to be recognised that there is no fast track to the elimination of low pay, that at some point minimum wages *can* have negative effects on employment, that a statutory wage floor is always a blunt instrument and that a subtler strategy is required.

To begin with, policymakers need a better diagnosis of *why* people are low paid. So far, the LPC has been invited to make recommendation on the level of the national minimum wage and on the impact of previous recommendations, with a view today of reaching the target of 60% of the median by 2020. What is missing from these terms of reference is a serious effort to assess what makes the UK different from other countries in terms of the incidence of low pay. The LPC could therefore be asked to investigate the *cause* of low wages, the *consequences* for the households affected (just what is it like to live on a low income?) and potential *cures* (what specific interventions beyond the national minimum wage are likely to make a difference?). One might say that, at present, the LPC is really a minimum wage commission. The task for the future is to enable the LPC to undertake the full range of functions suggested by its name.

It is likely that a wider investigation of this kind will identify low paid sectors that can afford to pay above the level of the current national minimum wage. It would be unwise to allow the LPC to set sectoral rates, not least because this would add another layer of complexity to the system. There is a strong case, however, for the LPC to develop some general principles for the measurement of affordability, which could then be discussed by unions and employers in that sector. One possibility would be for government to establish bodies analogous to the wages councils, which bring together employers and trade unions, with a view to developing joint strategies for skills development, skills utilisation and productivity.[7] It might also be possible, at the same time, for the parties to reach some agreement about a standard contract of employment, which could include a wage floor (consistent with the LPC's affordability criteria) to prevent the kind of exploitation experienced by workers with ZHCs.

Another measure worthy of consideration is the adoption of a new Fair Wages Resolution (FWR) by the House of Commons, consistent with Convention 98 of the International Labour Organisation on labour clauses in public contracts. The first FWR was adopted in 1891 by Lord Salisbury's Conservative government and it reflected the desire to ensure that the state, in all its manifestations, acted as a responsible client when procuring goods and services from the private sector. The most recent FWR was adopted by the postwar Labour government in 1946 and rescinded by Margaret Thatcher's government in 1983.

Essentially, the FWR required all government contractors to either observe the rates of pay specified in relevant collective agreements or observe the "general level", essentially the 'going rate' for a particular occupation in that locality, if no collective agreement was in operation. The FWR helped to eliminate bad employment practice in the government's supply chain and had a greater effect than any other single measure in encouraging the spread of collective bargaining across the UK economy (Kahn-Freund 1972).

A new FWR would have to be drafted to recognise the diminished status of trade unions in the UK today – in many cases it will be difficult to identify the relevant collective agreement. But where unions are recognised for collective bargaining a revived FWR will ensure that these negotiated rates cannot be undercut. If the government wishes, it could use the level of the living wage as the absolute minimum that an employer must pay to gain access to government contracts.

Pay, productivity and collective bargaining

We have also identified that those who are not low paid have also experienced serious wage problems in the last 25 years. For those in the bottom half of the wage distribution, pay growth became disconnected from productivity growth in the early 1990s. Since the crisis those at the median and below have seen little or no earnings growth and this stagnation is expected to continue over the next five years. So far as wage stagnation is concerned, a conventional economic explanation would draw attention to the UK's recent poor productivity record. It is axiomatic that if productivity is not rising that wages will not grow. No doubt this is true, but governments have been worrying away at the productivity question for decades, apparently to little effect.

Perhaps part of the answer lies in the analytical framework used by all governments, which has focused on five factors driving productivity growth: investment, innovation, skills, enterprise and competition. What is most interesting, perhaps, is that governments have been generally unwilling to look inside the 'black box' of the workplace at skills utilisation, the quality of management, the quality of work and the commitment of employees. If social democrats are serious about dealing with wage stagnation then part of the analysis must explain the relationship between productivity and all of these other elements. Most importantly, perhaps, it has to be recognised that workers possess a good deal of tacit knowledge about how to do their jobs more effectively – unlocking these 'secrets of production' could go some way towards redressing the UK's productivity deficit.

Addressing the pay-productivity decoupling is a more difficult and long-term exercise. Institutions appear to play an especially important role here, with domestic political choices being more influential than the impact of trade or technology on the structure of the wage distribution. Trade unions make a big difference in this context, which suggests that strengthening the unions is a necessary condition for social democratic advance. While this may be true, of course, it is important to ensure that institutions are entrenched, sustainable and are supported by employers as well as workers. That is why the proposal for the imposition of compulsory collective bargaining at sectoral level should be resisted (Hendy and Ewing 2017). The authors of this suggestion claim that they are simply drawing on the experience elsewhere in the EU, where employers can be made subject to a collective agreement (through so called extension mechanisms) even if they have not been a party to the original negotiations. In reality, however, this proposal would create a framework of compulsory collective bargaining that could undermine rather than enhance the effectiveness of trade unions. All the evidence shows that what makes unions resilient is membership strength and strong workplace organisation, where workplace representatives are trusted by members and respected by the employer.

That said, stronger trade unions would almost certainly lead to a fairer labour market in the UK. But unions, rather than relying on the state to do all the heavy lifting, need to be the agents of their own revival. The measures adumbrated above may help, but they are no panacea. Research over the last two decades has demonstrated that unions have an increasingly distant relationship with the majority of people at work – there are now more people who have *never* been members of trade unions than current members and ex-members combined (TUC 2003, Tait 2017). This raises profound questions for unions about both their essential purpose and the way they communicate that purpose to people at work today. Organising works councils as a route to organising workers will enable trade unions to establish their relevance and legitimacy with both workers and employers and, as has already been recorded, the information and consultation rights described above are arguably more extensive than anything currently available to trade unions through the normal machinery of collective bargaining.

Unions also have much to gain by embracing the vision of good work outlined at the beginning of this chapter, not least because what happens to workers from one day to the next is more important than episodic bargaining on pay and conditions. As the sociologist Alan Fox observed more than 50 years ago:

> The preoccupation with the unions' economic role in labour markets [wage formation] *has meant that **an even more important role*** [my emphasis] *has been neglected and insufficiently understood. This is the role of union organisation within the workplace in regulating managerial relations ie the exercise of management authority in deploying, organising and disciplining the labour force after it has been hired* (Fox 1966).

By emphasising questions of job quality unions will be doing no more than returning to their roots.

What about creative destruction? The importance of regional policy

While the proposals outlined above would represent a radical shift in corporate governance and employment relations policies, sceptical readers may be questioning whether, given the seriousness of the problems, any of these measures are sufficient to the task? Nothing that has been suggested so far speaks directly to the *consequences* of creative destruction, although the industrial democracy commitments may have some impact on the *process* of change. And none of these policies can guarantee that high-quality, well-paid work will be equally available to workers in every nation and region of the UK.

One might say that inclusive prosperity, where all workers benefit from economic growth, demands a more ambitious and comprehensive approach. Certainly, experience in continental Europe suggests that the mere existence of industrial democracy guarantees has done little to provide the security that citizens want and need under conditions of rapid change. It is essential to consider, therefore, what more might be done beyond the conventional social democratic prospectus.

We might find some inspiration in the experience of previous Labour governments. Harold Wilson's administration, from 1964–1970, had a well-developed approach to regional policy which, given the Labour leadership's revived interest in planning, may offer more guidance than anything that has happened in the last 20 years. There was a deliberate effort to encourage businesses to relocate from the prosperous south-east of England to those parts of the country that were struggling. A regional employment premium was available to manufacturing employers expanding their workforce in development areas – those parts of the country with lower incomes and higher unemployment, which covered around a fifth of the UK. Moreover, an effort was made to relocate new government-related organisations outside London – the Royal Mint went to south Wales, the Inland Revenue to Bootle and what is now the DVLA to Swansea. There were big increases in spending on regional infrastructure, with the aim of improving the productive potential of the economy and, less positively, direct subsidies to industries under pressure.

Some of these initiatives were very much of their time. One cannot imagine that direct cash payments to "uncompetitive" industries would find favour at any point in the political spectrum today. Nonetheless, the experience of the Wilson government highlights the necessity for a comprehensive, bold strategy, at the same time as it tells us that that macroeconomic policy sets the overall context for what is happening in the regions. Wilson's grand ambitions were deflected from their course by the weakness of the British economy when the government was elected in 1964, an overvalued exchange rate corrected by a hasty devaluation in 1967, and pressure on the government finances for the remainder of Labour's term in office. Perhaps the best lesson we can draw from this experience is that some element of planning, while useful to policymakers in framing the sphere of action, rarely survives contact with the real economy. Modesty, the principle that we sought to apply to predictions about the trajectory of technological developments, is equally applicable when we consider the possibility of planning for regional economic growth.

Of course major changes in the structures of regional governance have taken place since the 1960s, most notably, the creation of new institutions granting powers to city-region executive mayors. At present this is work in progress, but the potential exists for the emergence of strong political figures with national reputations who can act as a focus for policy development in their regions. It is the extent of devolution that creates the greatest contrast with the earlier period. Hitherto, everything was run from Whitehall, which meant that policies were broad-brush, slightly crude and not always adapted to local circumstances. It also meant that the potential of major relocations of government offices were not always fully exploited. Today, for example, there is a focus on the role of "anchor institutions" in driving forward the process of economic development. A university or a leading teaching hospital, for example, attracts a large number of professionals and students to a locality. This means that more money is being spent in the local economy than would otherwise be the case. Affluent middle-class professionals bring in their wake the development of a range of private services in leisure and hospitality that create opportunities in the local economy. Moreover, anchor institutions can develop local supply chains and build the capacity of local economies to provide the services required. One weakness in the Wilson government's approach was that it failed effectively to leverage the role of government offices in the regions. Relocating activities from London created isolated islands of decent employment in what was otherwise an ocean of decline.

Despite the earlier criticisms of Labour's 2017 manifesto, the proposals on regional infrastructure were well developed and credible. They enjoy widespread support across the party and create no deep ideological divisions between left and right. The same might be said for the commitment to create regional development banks on the German model, which would provide support for businesses that struggle to access capital through conventional means.

Improving skill levels and levels of educational attainment must also be part of the story if previously disadvantaged areas are to reap the benefits of investment in the future. There is a case for increasing spending on early years provision too, since what happens before the age of five can affect success in compulsory education. It is possible to go further and say that access to lifelong learning, however delivered, is essential if all citizens are to be equipped with the capabilities they need to choose lives that they have reason to value.

The real political challenge is to offer people hope that practical steps are being taken to address the inequalities in regional (and sub-regional) prosperity and opportunity. Developing effective policies is essential but having a compelling narrative is important too. People must be convinced that something important will change in their community and that prospect of improvement must be real. This means that the condition of the physical environment matters too. Pat McFadden MP puts it like this:

> *The investment famine in some of our smaller cities has been ignored for far too long. . . . No wonder people feel they do not have a stake in our national story when contaminated land, old mineshafts and derelict buildings stand as barriers to development and renewal* (McFadden 2017).

Physical decay and dereliction of what once was a vibrant industrial community can obviously inspire the nostalgic impulse that lies beneath the surface of populism. People are angry, are looking for someone to blame and want to 'go back to the way the world used to be'; it is not irrational to believe, in some communities, that the past was better than the present. Nonetheless, social democracy stands in direct opposition to this backward-looking gospel of hopelessness. We believe that the state can act, take responsibility and seek to eliminate these evils. Indeed, the willingness to take responsibility is a constitutive element of all progressive politics. Conservatives, on the other hand, seek to dispense with the role of the state believing that, in the long run, the market will work to produce an optimal outcome. The history of the last 40 years has tested that belief to destruction. The time has come to move on.

QUESTIONS FOR THE LEFT
Challenges for the 2020s

[T]he essence of all faith, it seems to be . . . is that man's [sic]
life can be and will be better; that man's greatest enemies, in the
forms in which they now exist – the forms we see on every hand
of fear, hatred, slavery, cruelty, poverty and need – can be con-
quered and destroyed... To believe that new monsters will arise
as vicious as the old, to believe that the great Pandora's box of
human frailty, once opened, will never show a diminution of its
ugly swarm, is to help, by just that much, to make it so forever.

Thomas Wolfe, *You Can't Go Home Again* (1940)

OPTIMISM; A RECIPE FOR SUCCESS?

A consistent theme throughout this volume has been the identifica-
tion of social democracy with the belief that present evils can be
eliminated (or at least ameliorated) by the intelligent intervention of
government, supported by wider social movements. Only representative governments, using the authority and legitimacy conferred on
them by citizens, can intervene to constrain accumulations of unaccountable private power – whether held by individuals, corporations
or other social actors. Only governments have the wherewithal to
tackle poverty, discrimination and inequality. Only governments,

representing a free people, can take the steps needed to ensure that the maximum practical liberty is available to all citizens. The effectiveness of social democracy therefore depends on an active and accountable state, which has to be fit for purpose to deliver the ends in view.

This may sound a little bureaucratic but it is important nonetheless. More readily understood, perhaps, is that social democracy, or progressive politics more generally defined, is most successful when it demonstrates an acute understanding of the problems perplexing citizens today *and* offers an optimistic prospect for the future. We can see this in Roosevelt's victory in 1932, when the New Deal was exemplified by the song of the moment: "happy days are here again". We can see it too in the song of Bill Clinton's successful 1992 campaign: "don't stop thinking about tomorrow". And it is obviously part of the story of Labour's success in 1945, where the manifesto was entitled *Let Us Face the Future*, in 1964, where Harold Wilson allied a programme of technological modernisation to a rejection of "grouse moor conservatism", and in 1997, where New Labour's programme was accompanied by the (somewhat irritating) theme, "things can only get better".

We might conclude too that Labour's unexpectedly good performance in 2017 was another example of the same phenomenon. Jeremy Corbyn and his colleagues were presenting a hopeful future to the nation – ending austerity, regenerating depressed regions, making the economy work for everybody. The Tory mistake was to present a programme that offered more retrenchment, reductions in public spending and what became known as the dementia tax. This observation does not negate our earlier criticisms of Labour's 2015 programme, which looked to the past for inspiration and would have proved problematic, at best, to implement in government. But the 2017 result proves an enduring political truth: optimism generally beats pessimism.

Despite the supposed boldness of Labour's 2017 manifesto, the programme presented was, arguably, a systematic evasion of the most pressing issues facing the nation. Very little was said, for example, about the unavoidably difficult fiscal policy choices that will be required, about climate change, about the ageing of the UK population, about practical measures (rather than rhetoric) to address income inequality, about the appropriate boundary between the public and private sectors, about the capacity of the British state and the need for a new constitutional settlement or, beyond some judicious fudging, about Brexit and the UK's role in the world. We have already observed that Labour is most successful when it has a well-developed programme, with clear priorities and a strategy for the creation of new, durable institutions to entrench progressive goals. Assuming that the party has the luxury of time, there is a perfect opportunity to develop compelling responses to each of these challenges.

The purpose of the following discussion is not to set out a detailed menu again – that would be the height of arrogance – but to describe in a little more detail the nature of the problems that Labour needs to solve, relating this exercise to our earlier discussion about equality, liberty and the need to make an assessment of what people can do with their freedom. Readers will note two major omissions: very little is said about either housing or education policy. In part that is because the issues are so complex they demand treatment beyond the scope of this volume, but it is also because others have rather greater expertise than the present author and I have no wish to try people's patience by making poorly developed proposals. So far as housing is concerned, the victims of the Grenfell Tower tragedy deserve more than a few short paragraphs on the desirability of a new housing investment programme.

CLIMATE CHANGE

Many readers may be either irritated or enraged by the material presented so far in this volume, and none more so than those who, quite legitimately, argue that nothing has been said so far about climate change, the greatest existential threat to the future of humanity.

To that charge I plead guilty, but offer in mitigation the observation that unless Labour can win a general election and govern success-fully, the UK will make limited progress in addressing the most perplexing of all global challenges.

It is true that the Paris Agreement contains impressive commit-ments from global leaders, but we might reasonably ask whether this has penetrated the consciousness of democratic electorates, where the majority of citizens are concerned about more quotidian matters. Before the Brexit referendum result, the UK was able to participate in the global conversation as part of the EU. Now, post-Brexit, the UK's voice will be diminished to the level of inaudibility, when confronted with global behemoths like the US, China or India.

Nonetheless, the UK still requires genuinely inspiring political leadership which, following our earlier analysis, is honest about the problem but presents an optimistic outlook – an environmentally sustainable economic and social model that guarantees security, liberty and decent incomes for all. Moreover, responding effectively to a less forgiving environment will not be achieved by nostalgic appeals to a better yesterday or to the idea that Britain is at its best when it stands alone. The rising tides and more uncertain climatic conditions demand openness and international collaboration, and that means the UK should remain as close as possible to the EU on climate change policy, particularly now that the US has abandoned global leadership.

Despite all the rhetoric about the changing labour market, the transformational potential of technology and the rise of the robots, it is climate change that is likely to be most disruptive to established patterns of life and work. Trade unions have understood this better than most, with their call for a just transition, recognising that there may be significant industrial restructuring, that some jobs will dis-appear entirely and that workers will need support to find a secure place in a very different world.

A consistent theme of this volume has been the need for better policy integration and co-ordination – labour market policy, indus-trial policy, regional policy and a programme of public investment must all be pulling in the same direction. Tackling the challenge of climate change could play an indispensable role in this process, acting as an organising principle and setting out clear goals – meeting the UK's carbon reduction targets while maintaining inclusive prosperity – against which progress can be measured.

It would be wrong to think that responding to climate change must be a Labour government's *only* priority; that would be absurd. But climate change sets the context for everything else that appears in this volume. It is something of a challenge to choose a life that one has reason to value when the water is lapping at your knees.

IT'S THE ECONOMY, STUPID

It has been an article of faith amongst progressives, since Bill Clinton's election in 1992, that a practical prospectus for the economy is the foundation stone of electoral victory for all progressive parties. It does not matter how disaffected electors might be by conservative failures to invest in public services or support the most disadvantaged. If the principal party of the left has failed to present a responsible and credible economic policy then electoral victory will prove elusive.

Once again, some supporters of Labour's current leadership will argue that this logic has broken down in the post-crisis, post-Brexit referendum period. There is no need to be responsible in the New Labour sense because the electorate have recognised the awful impact of austerity policies and are desperate for an alternative. There may be a grain of truth in this argument, but it seems to take no account of the woeful Tory campaign, the weakness of Theresa May's leadership or the deep divisions inside the Conservative party about the UK's post-Brexit trajectory.

Of course, it is worth recalling that most people expected Labour to be wiped off the electoral map in the 2017 general election. The result may have been surprising, but Labour failed to win and still lags behind the Tories on all measures of economic competence and credibility. Given the parlous condition of the government, this does not augur well for the future. A tired and divided Tory party should not be outpolling the opposition.

An independent review of Labour's performance in the wake of the 2015 defeat highlighted three specific areas of weakness, all of which have yet to be addressed: the electorate did not trust Labour to manage the economy effectively; there was a widespread belief that Labour was "soft" on welfare and supported the feckless and undeserving; many working-class voters were concerned about the impact of immigration on their communities and believed that Labour was in favour of open borders (Cruddas et al. 2016).

These findings go some way towards explaining the 2017 result too, most notably the fall in the Labour vote in previously safe seats (Bishop Auckland, Ashfield) and losses in heartland areas (Mansfield, Derbyshire North East, Stoke-on-Trent South, Walsall North). Labour was winning votes from groups that supported open-ness, cosmopolitanism and membership of the EU and losing votes amongst people whose interests the Labour party was established to defend. If anything, the 2017 result confirms the fracturing of the Labour coalition and suggests that British politics is becoming mired in the culture wars that have done such damage in the US Labour's task, therefore, is to rebuild its electoral coalition by developing an agenda that recognises the weaknesses in the party's position, without endorsing the argument that only fiscal conservatism and tough immigration controls can secure electoral victory.

The New Labour period before the 1997 election offers some guidance about how the front bench might proceed. Gordon Brown had made public commitments to hold debt at a stable and prudent level through the adoption of two fiscal rules: the golden rule required that borrowing would only be used to fund public investment over the course of the economic cycle; the sustainable debt rule required overall government indebtedness to be held at a stable and prudent level, defined as no more than 40% of GDP. Both rules were apparently abandoned as a result of the global financial crisis but they had, until the early 2000s, given the chancellor a high level of credibility. Institutions lending to the government could be certain about Labour's intentions, there was no doubt that the Treasury was committed to prudence and the collapse of the banking system was an exceptional event – even those predicting a crash failed to foresee the profundity of the crisis.

Arguably, Labour needs to make a similar statement today to demonstrate seriousness of purpose in the management of the public finances. Something like the golden rule needs to be readopted, demonstrating Labour's commitment to borrow either to improve the productive potential of the economy or to recapitalise public services in need of investment. Recurrent spending commitments will need to be funded from taxation, which means that Labour must be clear about the how revenue is to be raised. It is likely that the tax burden will therefore increase and, if the tax base is to be sustainable, then marginal rates of income tax for those on middle incomes will have to rise too. The common sense of the New Labour period was that the electorate were resistant to any rises in income tax, which limited the possibilities for social democratic advance. To a degree this was and remains true, but Gordon Brown did raise the level of national insurance contributions to fund extra spending on the NHS, without any adverse impact on electoral Labour's performance.

As with climate change, this is another area where bold leadership is required. Experience proves that people are willing to pay more tax if they support the uses to which the additional revenues will be put. This means in turn that Labour must make the case for the proper funding of its programme, must explain how the money will be spent and must avoid the seductive, populist belief that somebody else ('the rich', 'greedy bankers', 'rapacious companies') can pick up the bill. No doubt sceptical readers will demand a little more precision about how much will be borrowed, how much should be raised in tax and who will have to pay. These are legitimate questions for the front bench at the time of the next general election but there is no need to answer them today. Labour needs some agreed principles to guide the development of policy, which is the purpose of this discussion. The details can come later.

Gordon Brown's response to the global crisis was classically Keynesian, continuing to fund spending by borrowing more when tax revenues were falling. But Keynes also suggested that the public finances should be repaired once the economy has returned to a stable growth path. Keynesian economics does not demand a commitment to ever-higher levels of government indebtedness or unrestrained government borrowing. On the other hand, austerity, adopted by the coalition government following the 2010 general election, was precisely the wrong approach at the wrong time. A nascent recovery was choked off with entirely predictable consequences: slower growth, stagnant wages, public services under pressure and, for the poorest households, a decline in real incomes. The consequences of austerity are visible everywhere: winter pressures in the NHS, local authorities implementing emergency budget cuts to control spending, homeless people on the streets, reductions in benefit levels. Continuing on this path will do lasting damage to the UK's economic and social fabric and, when combined with the consequences of Brexit, will make the nation poorer rather than more prosperous.

Nonetheless, if we are good Keynesians there has to be some commitment to restoring the public finances to order – with surpluses in good years to allow for more borrowing when the economy hits a bump in the road. Labour may be committed to rolling back austerity, but it still has to explain how the deficit is to be reduced and how debt can be repaid. Part of the answer lies in a programme of public investment – infrastructure spending, support for science, regional development banks – which should foster a higher rate of growth, generating a higher level of tax receipts for the Treasury in the medium to long term. But even a programme of public investment requires a prioritisation of projects, not least to avoid the accusation that money is being spent unwisely. Moreover, all investments take time to generate anticipated revenues and a Labour government will have to make judgements about public spending immediately after a general election. Ending austerity may be the goal but this can only be achieved if the government is clear about priorities – of which the choice between support for early years provision or a reduction in university tuition fees is an obvious example. Not every Tory cut can be immediately reversed, no matter how devoutly we might all wish for that outcome.

Perhaps the best conclusion we can reach is that there are no right answers to these questions. Progressive politics is invariably impaled on the horns of a dilemma: on the one hand the bold promises (or at least the bold rhetoric) needed to win an election; on the other the realities of limited resources and difficult fiscal policy choices. In the current environment the public seem to have a low tolerance threshold for dissimulation and, while optimism about the future is essential to the left's success, making durable change demands that optimism is tempered by a willingness to accept the real constraints on a government's room for manoeuvre.

Beyond these principles for action (the fiscal rules, honesty about difficult choices) Labour has to demonstrate that it understands how a capitalist economy works – its advantages and disadvantages – with a particular emphasis on the realities of creative destruction. We have already considered the case for more state intervention through regional and industrial policies to ensure that citizens have the capabilities they need to cope with disruptive change, but policy can go further in shaping both the pace and trajectory of change.

Finally, it is essential for Labour to recognise the truth that markets have distinct advantages. Competition can sometimes be wasteful, but it is also a source of innovation, delivering new products and services to fulfil wants of which people may have been ignorant. Markets offer citizens diversity, choice and a wide range of commodities that respond to highly differentiated preferences. Moreover, markets, when they work well, are efficient institutions for the allocation of capital as well as goods and services.

The task for Labour is to be clear what action can and should be taken when markets do not work efficiently. In some cases the answer may be regulation, to protect consumers against exploitation. In others it may be a matter of breaking up monopolies or concentrations of market power and, as we shall see in the next section, in certain circumstances the state may wish to take an industry into public ownership. The important point is for policymakers to have *all* these policy instruments at their disposal. An essential part of Labour's case is that government intervention can make a real difference to the conduct of corporations and the quality of the work available to workers.

The extension of public ownership?

Straight-talking, honest politics is required in relation to the vexed question of public ownership too. Labour's 2017 manifesto contained commitments to a rolling renationalisation of the railways as franchises expire; to regain control of energy supply networks with a transition to a publicly owned, decentralised energy system; to create a network of regional, publicly owned water companies; and, to renationalise Royal Mail at the earliest opportunity. The privatisation of the railways is almost universally acknowledged to have been a mistake, with members across Labour's ideological spectrum favouring some form of public ownership. Whether the same is true for the other industries on Labour's list is an open question, to which, surprisingly, there may be no right answer.

Perhaps the first point to make is that the boundary between the public and the private sector has generally been determined pragmatically rather than ideologically. One might begin with the simple observation that, historically, the public provision of water, electricity, gas and telecommunications reflected the inability of the private sector to deliver the services in question. But the line is not so easily drawn as that.

In the US, for example, water utilities remain in largely public ownership, with the experience of private provision sometimes being characterised by corruption and poor performance. In France, the management of water resources has been in private hands for most of the last century, but there is evidence of a trend towards direct municipal ownership and control today, of which Paris is a good example. And in the UK, water was largely a public responsibility until Margaret Thatcher's government privatised the industry in 1989.[1] Across much of the rest of Europe water is in public ownership and control. In Uruguay, a constitutional amendment was passed in 2004 preventing the privatisation of the industry.

In other sectors, the trend is decisively in the direction of private ownership – this is certainly true for airlines and for telecommunications and it is notable that Jeremy Corbyn and John McDonnell have not identified either BT or British Airways as candidates for renationalisation. Yet even here the story is not straightforward. In New Zealand, for example, Helen Clark's Labour government took control of the national airline in 2001, when the business almost collapsed following a disastrous takeover of the Australian airline Ansett. Air New Zealand has remained in largely public ownership under subsequent centre-right administrations, with the government continuing to own 53% of the shares in the business. Nonetheless, it is an open question whether, in the absence of a catastrophic business failure, the New Zealand government would have considered public ownership at all[2].

Most developed countries that had taken ownership and control of industries like mining and steelmaking have now returned these activities to the private sector. A notable counter-example is Codelco, the largest copper mining company in the world, which is owned by the government of Chile, having been nationalised by Salvador Allende's socialist administration in 1971. Despite the commitment to free market economics, the Pinochet dictatorship made no effort to return the mines to their previous, largely American, owners. Public ownership of Codelco is a matter of political consensus in Chile today.

It is worth recalling, perhaps, that public ownership is not necessarily a matter of taking control of entire industries. Tony Crosland was, until the end of his life, an enthusiast for the idea of competitive public enterprise for, as he put it:

> *"[T]he establishment (either from scratch or by takeover) of state companies or joint ventures to compete with private enterprise – to act as highly competitive price-leaders and pace-setters, provide a*

yardstick for efficiency, support the government's investment plans,
and above all produce a better product or service" (Crosland 1974).

Public intervention in this form is designed to *intensify* competition, one might even say, in Schumpeterian terms, to *accelerate* the process of creative destruction. We are worlds away, however, from a monolithic public bureaucracy or a subsidised basket case business that can only survive with government support.

Another argument used to justify public ownership is that these activities are natural monopolies; markets cannot work without competition and it simply is not possible to create competitive markets in these industries. This was certainly part of the case made against the privatisation of all the utilities in the UK. But contrary to the critics' expectations, there is at least some competition in the provision of both electricity and gas today – the difficulty is that consumers are baffled by the choice between complex competing tariffs.

The complexity of these tariffs is a fine example of the information asymmetries we discussed in Chapter 1, where the provider of a service uses jargon and obfuscation to bamboozle the consumer, preventing the market from working effectively because the consumer never has the transparent information needed to make an accurate judgement about where their best interests might lie. This argument, that the market cannot work efficiently because consumers always have imperfect information, may constitute a better case for public ownership than the 'natural monopoly' argument, although it is also consistent with more decisive regulatory intervention as an alternative to nationalisation.

Finally, many democratic socialists have historically taken the view that the expansion of public ownership is an indicator of the extent of progressive advance. In part, this is because capitalism has always been viewed as inherently exploitative, but it is also a result of the belief that governments must have direct control of the commanding heights of the economy if they are to plan for full employment. Expressed crudely, achieving strong economic performance is too important to be left to the capitalists.

The arguments used in the 2017 manifesto are some distance from this ambitious strategy, focusing instead on the loss of democratic control associated with privatisation and the disadvantages experienced by consumers who are paying more than they should for these basic services. The argument about democratic control is not entirely convincing, since individual citizens had no more influence over the behaviour of a public corporation in the past than they do over a privatised utility today. Nor is it clear that a direct return to public ownership is the best route to lower prices. All of these utilities are regulated, they all have their prices scrutinised by a public authority and they could all be prevented, for example, from subjecting consumers to what can only be described as price gouging[3].

Renationalising the railways will be cost-free, because the franchises can simply be taken back under public control at the expiry of the contracts with the private provider. More problems might be anticipated in relation to water, energy and Royal Mail, where compensation will be required for the owners; shareholders are expecting to be given government bonds to the value of their shareholding. In other words, taking these industries back into public ownership will increase the volume of debt on the government's balance sheet and leave fewer resources available for investment in other priorities. It may seem a crude characterisation, but compensating shareholders will mean less investment in the regions, fewer resources for infrastructure or housing, and a less effective industrial policy.

Perhaps the boundary between public and private sector today is fixed more as a matter of path dependency than ideology. Once an industry is under public ownership and control, powerful forces will resist privatisation; similarly, once an industry has been privatised, equally powerful forces will resist renationalisation. All governments can do is make a pragmatic judgement at the time, reflecting the resources available and their scale of priorities. Given the other demands for public investment, it is not entirely clear that renationalising the water utilities, energy or Royal Mail should be a matter of urgency for a Labour government, although, of course, this does not rule out some consideration of the status of these industries in the future.

DEMOGRAPHICS: THE AGEING
POPULATION AND IMMIGRATION

It is generally recognised that one of Theresa May's biggest mistakes in the 2017 general election campaign was to suggest that people might be compelled to use their housing wealth to fund their care in old age. All opposition parties made much of the proposal for a dementia tax and there can be no doubt that it did real damage to the Conservatives' prospects of winning a majority in the House of Commons. A dispassionate assessment would suggest that the prime minister was heroic in addressing an undeniably serious issue but had a poor understanding of the likely public reaction. While an undeniable gift to the opposition, the progress of the discussion during the general election almost certainly diminished public understanding of the choices facing the nation.

The British population is ageing. By 2046 one in four citizens will be over the age of 65 – in 1976 the figure was closer to one in seven. Life expectancy is rising too. According to official projections, women born in 2015 can expect to live to the age of 83 (four years more than in 1991) and men born in the same year can expect to live until the age of 80 (ONS 2017). Inevitably, these demographic shifts raise questions about the financing of the state pension system, the level of public support available for the care of the elderly and the implications for the NHS of dealing with a larger number of very elderly people in the final stages of their lives.

Labour may have condemned the Tories for the dementia tax, but the 2017 manifesto also contained proposals for the financing of care for the elderly, referring specifically to wealth taxes, an employer care contribution or a "social care levy". Beyond this, the manifesto was silent, although the use of wealth taxes to fund social care does sound a little like a dementia tax. It is also noteworthy that the manifesto referred to the importance of achieving a cross-party consensus, presumably of the kind that has been achieved in relation to compulsory pension saving, where all the major parties now accept the case for mandatory contributions from employers and workers.

The most obvious policy response to the ageing of the population has been the gradual increase in the state pension age. Under current plans the state pension age will rise to 66 in 2020 and 67 in 2028. A further increase to 68 is planned sometime between 2037 and 2039. These reforms have reduced the extent of the increase in the dependency ratio – the percentage of people over retirement age as compared with the percentage of people of working age – but a dramatic change is still being forecast (Figure 4.1). For most of the period from 1980 to the end of the twentieth century, for example, there were 300 people in retirement for every 1000 people of working age. By 2039, there will be 365 people in retirement for every 1000 people of working age. On current trends, the dependency ratio will rise further after the end of the forecast period.

From one standpoint the policy looks entirely rational, but some citizens, especially in disadvantaged communities, might consider

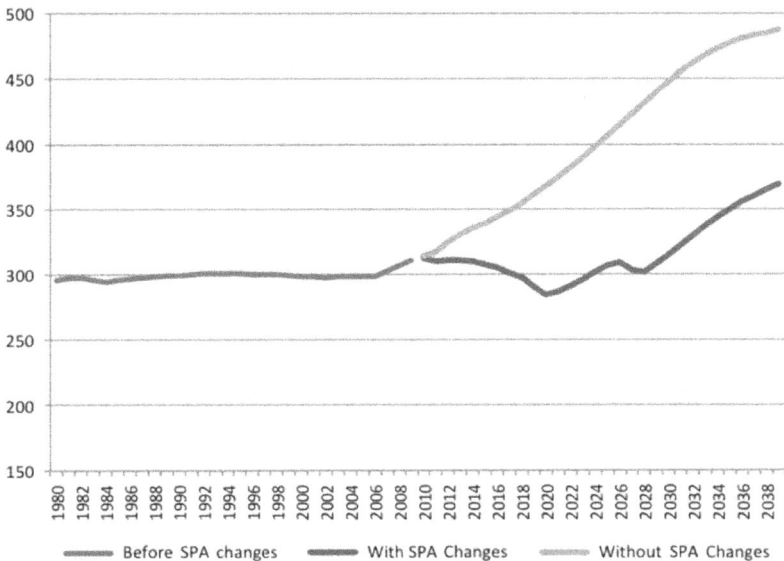

Figure 4.1 **Old age dependency ratio 1980–2039 (number of people aged 65+ to each 1,000 people of working age).** *Source:* ONS – Population projections are from 2014.

their treatment to be unfair. It is clear, for example, that those in the bottom quarter of the income distribution have shorter lives than those who are more affluent (Marmot 2010) Indeed, in the *most* disadvantaged communities, there is some evidence to show that average life expectancy for men has fallen in recent times. Even if this is an isolated phenomenon, it is undeniable that those with lower incomes are much less likely to enjoy good health after the age of 60 (Marmot 2010). In Sweden, increases in the state retirement age are linked to increases in the life expectancy of the bottom quartile. There is a strong case for the adoption of a similar policy in the UK.

The population projections used by all the recent enquiries into the affordability of the UK's pension system have made assumptions about population growth and immigration derived from the UK's continued membership of the EU. In a post-Brexit world, most of these assumptions will no longer be valid, which means that the government has two options: either, it can accept that the dependency ratio will rise, imposing a heavier burden of taxation on citizens of working age; or, the government can allow a rise in immigration from outside the EU, to compensate for the ending of free movement. Both options look unpalatable from a Conservative standpoint; the first because it requires higher taxes; and the second because, contrary to the desires of many Brexit supporters, it permits a continued high level of immigration.

What has been missing from the national conversation so far is honesty about these issues. Sustaining economic growth requires access to people of working age who can fill vacancies as and when they arise. Without a supply of labour from overseas, whether from the EU or elsewhere, everybody, both pensioners and people of working age, will be poorer.

The second element of the pensions consensus is that everybody should (in partnership with their employers) be saving more for retirement. Contributions are set to rise from 5% today to 8% in April 2019 (3% from the employer, 5% from the employee), but there is a serious question whether increases on this scale can deliver an adequate supplement to the basic state pension. It is generally accepted that around 15% of pay needs to be saved throughout a working life to deliver a decent, secure, retirement income. No doubt employers will complain about any increase in the compulsory contribution level, but the choice facing them is clear: either pay higher pensions contributions today or face higher corporate taxes tomorrow. Labour has an opportunity to show leadership in reshaping the UK's pensions system, making the case that there is no contradiction between affordability and fairness so long as a comprehensive approach is adopted recognising the linkages between pensions policy, the quality of work, inequality of incomes and the costs of sickness to the NHS. A healthier working-age population can expect to enjoy better health in retirement, which confirms the pursuit of greater income equality as a valuable instrument in achieving a wide variety of desirable social outcomes.

INEQUALITY, REDISTRIBUTION AND THE WELFARE STATE

We have already affirmed the importance of action by the state to provide a system of social insurance that protects people against the vicissitudes of life. That is what the postwar welfare state was designed to do and, despite weaknesses in dealing with creative destruction, the model was relatively successful. Social democrats should not abandon their commitment to either social insurance or income transfers to households with low incomes. But it is important to establish a principled basis for policy development, both to refute the argument from the right that all welfare spending supports the lazy, feckless or undeserving and to restore the faith of former Labour voters that the social security system works for them.

To begin with, Labour should ban the word 'welfare' from its lexicon and start talking again about social security, emphasising that the state is providing a system of insurance against the setbacks that we all face in life. John Hills has already shown us how to make persuasive arguments of this kind, with an appeal to solidarity – *everybody* uses the system as a child, a parent and a pensioner – to counteract the notion that 'welfare' is for someone else (Hills 2015).

Second, a serious effort must be made to rebuild the contributory elements of the system. The idea of 'something for something' or 'you pay in when you can and you take out when you need to' has been inherent in the design of policy since the time of Asquith's Liberal government. Labour's expansion of social security in the postwar period built on these foundations but avoided some difficult decisions that still haunt policymakers today (Timmins 1995). The government was concerned, for example, that the levels of national insurance proposed by Beveridge were higher than many voters would tolerate, so both contributions and the benefits available were pitched lower than originally envisaged. A natural consequence of this decision was that many households struggled to survive on the contributory benefits alone, meaning that the means-tested parts of the system were bearing a heavier burden than intended. Moreover, the system has always struggled to reconcile adequate support for housing costs with the notion of social insurance – housing benefit has always been means-tested.

The reality today is that the support offered by the social security system is inadequate. Many people who lose their jobs are surprised to find that the contributory element of jobseeker's allowance (JSA) delivers a less than generous £73.10 per week; in real terms this sum is worth half as much as the comparable unemployment benefit in 1975. Of course, the non-contributory elements of JSA are now part of the universal credit (UC) system, the problems with which have been well documented elsewhere.

To argue for a contribution-based system of social insurance with more generous levels of benefits may seem counter-intuitive as a response to the diagnosis in the Cruddas review of the 2015 defeat; less generosity was popular and more coercion welcome. But what Labour needs to do is transform the terms of the public conversation. If the focus is invariably on the costs of 'welfare' then Labour will always be running to catch the Conservatives' coat tails. If, on the other hand, the discussion is couched in terms of the insurance against risk available to *all* citizens then Labour has an opportunity to seize the initiative.

The important point here, of course, is that access to out-of-work benefits, even though dependent on contribution, should not be unconditional. This is the lesson of the Nordic labour market models that proved successful before the global financial crisis. It was the judicious mix of generous benefits, tight job search obligations (with penalties for non-compliance) *and* investment in skills that delivered the positive outcomes.

Greater clarity is required in describing the nature of the support available to those who lose their jobs. For much of the postwar period it was assumed that unemployment was a frictional phenomenon; people would find work fairly quickly. All the government needed to do was offer short-term income replacement and use macroeconomic policy to maintain full employment. Once mass unemployment arrived in the 1980s the focus shifted to 'activation', with sanctions applied to those who failed to comply with job search conditions. Now, however, there is a strong case for saying that the centre of attention must shift to capabilities – does somebody who is unemployed have the wherewithal to find a good job and keep it? There is also a case for more flexibility in the system at regional, sub-regional and local level, with Jobcentre Plus collaborating with the city-region mayors to develop strategies tailored to the immediate needs of those without work. 'Something for something' means getting worthwhile support when you are in difficulty.

Our earlier discussion noted that income inequality rose significantly in the 1980s and that nothing has been done to reverse the change subsequently. Equally troubling, perhaps, particularly in the context of the discussion about the dementia tax, is the slow but inexorable rise that has taken place in *wealth* inequality in recent years. The most recent analysis suggests, in crude terms, that the top 10% of the population hold a very large percentage of the nation's assets (Figure 4.2).

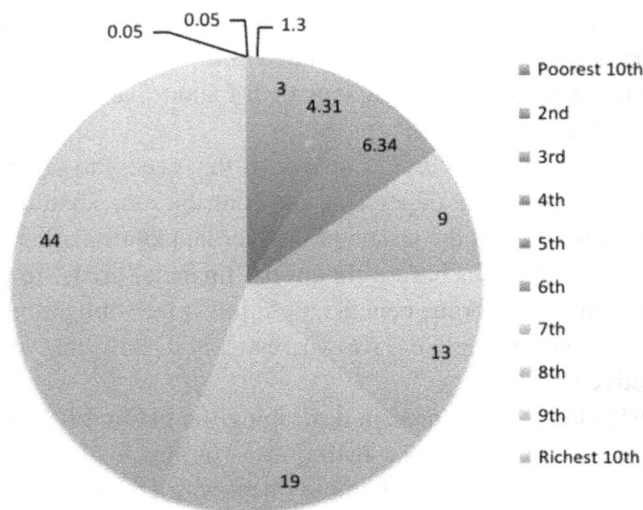

Figure 4.2   Wealth inequality in the UK July 2014–June 2016 (% total wealth held by each income decile). *Source:* ONS, Total Wealth: Wealth in Great Britain.

By any standards this looks like an unjustifiable distribution of affluence. We can see why, following Rawls, such concentrations of wealth can undermine democracy, because money buys access to power. And we can see, following Amartya Sen, that almost anything is available for those in the top three deciles (they hold almost 75% of total wealth), while the remaining 70% of the population struggle to acquire the capabilities they need to choose lives they have reason to value.

Much of this concentration of wealth is attributable to the dysfunction of the UK's housing market and the problem may be about to get worse as the immediate postwar generation begins to die, passing on their accumulated housing assets to their families. A further concentration of capital in fewer and fewer hands will intensify the divisions between classes and regions described in this volume. For social democrats the situation is intolerable and the case for intervention irresistible. We should recall, perhaps, that one of the priorities identified by Tony Crosland in *The Future of Socialism* was an assault on inherited wealth, which cannot said to be deserved by its recipients. More recently Will Hutton has proposed a radical recasting of inheritance tax or, as he describes it, a "we share in your good luck tax", to prevent the continued accumulation of wealth by those who are already at the top of the distribution (Hutton 2015).

Those with longer memories may recall that Gordon Brown got into some difficulty over inheritance tax shortly after he became prime minister. The notion that Labour should say *anything* bold on the taxation of either income or wealth seems to have died sometime after the 1992 general election defeat. It is true that any attempt to tax inherited wealth will be attacked by the Conservatives on the grounds that Labour is interfering again, preventing people from disposing of their property as they see fit. But there is a world of difference between leaving a modest terrace to one's children and doing the same with a London townhouse, a country cottage and a Tuscan villa. Only the top 30% of the population will be affected by Hutton's proposal, with most people remaining confident that their modest holdings will be untouched. Nonetheless, the real problem lies at the top of the distribution, and it is at the top, perhaps, that attention should be focused.

A consistent theme of this volume is that inherited wealth is incompatible with common sense notions of fairness and, in any event, the 'liberty' to dispose of one's property as one sees fit is far from absolute in a democracy. We should recall Isaiah Berlin's dictum that freedom for the wolves often means death to the sheep. It is entirely reasonable, therefore, to initiate an informed discussion about what ought to be done about concentrations of wealth, not in pursuit of a politics of envy but, following Rawls, to take the action necessary to secure equal citizenship. To address these questions openly and honestly is constitutive of what it means to live in a pluralist democracy.

THE STATE AS PROVIDER OR FUNDER OF CITIZENSHIP GOODS: THE LIMITS OF MARKETS

Both Jeremy Corbyn and John McDonnell are known for their opposition to privatisation, which is generally interpreted as a rejection of the approach adopted by both Labour and Conservative governments to the reform of public services. Given recent experience – the failure of private prisons, the collapse of Carillion and the profit warnings issued by Capita – one can understand that a degree of scepticism is warranted. But it is important to be clear about Labour's alternative which, all too often, appears rooted in the belief that *any* private sector involvement in the delivery of public services is wrong in principle and must therefore be resisted. This somewhat unsophisticated approach will be difficult to apply in government and, once again, could lead to disappointment and disaffection. It is important to be clear, therefore, about the meaning of privatisation, which has a number of manifestations, all of which are different in their nature and quality.

Privatisation

To begin with, there is the straightforward transfer of an industry that was in public ownership into private hands. This, initially, is what the Conservatives meant when they talked about privatisation and they justified the policy by arguing that the government had no business owning activities that could, quite happily, be run as private concerns in competitive markets, of which British Telecom and British Airways are two obvious examples. The Tory case for private ownership might be viewed as the obverse of the Corbynistas' case for public ownership, but both standpoints are too ideological and fail to reflect the need for pragmatic judgement. Sometimes, as Edward Heath's government discovered in 1971 when it nationalised Rolls-Royce, even Conservatives are persuaded by the argument for nationalisation, albeit in crisis conditions.

Contracting out

More insidious, perhaps, is the second form of privatisation, the contracting out of particular activities or services to a private sector provider. In this case the state is acting as the commissioner of the service, which is tax-funded, where the consumers of the service are ordinary citizens. During the Thatcher period local government became the test bed for this approach, with the introduction of competitive tendering for construction-related services, refuse collection, street cleaning, building cleaning, school meals provision and parks maintenance, rapidly followed by a range of back office, administrative services.

The principled justification for the policy went much wider than local government, however, and was founded on the belief that public services are inherently inefficient and will always benefit from a healthy dose of competition and private sector management. On this view public servants are just as much motivated by self-interest as those working in private businesses (Le Grand 2003, 2008). Because there is no competition to act as an incentive for either innovation or responsiveness, public services will always prove inferior to their counterparts in the private sector. All talk of the 'public service ethos' is used to mask the desire of producers to run the service for their own convenience. The case for competitive tendering and private sector involvement is therefore irresistible if governments are serious about protecting public services from 'producer capture'. Moreover, the case is applicable to *all* public services, to health, education and, in some variants, to the provision of policy advice by civil servants. Why, some supporters of this standpoint ask, should Whitehall mandarins have a job for life, when senior consultants from McKinsey, PwC or Deloitte may have rather more to offer? Why not put the provision of policy advice out to competitive tender every five years? Everything that can be subjected to market processes should be subjected to market processes and if markets cannot be established then policymakers ought to look for market-like mechanisms (quasi-markets) to achieve the same ends.

The idea of competition as a universal good inspired the Health and Social Care Act 2012 that would, in its original incarnation, have transformed the NHS into a regulated utility like the privatised water companies. The same cast of mind continues to inspire higher education policy today, where universities are in direct competition with each other for students and a market system is in operation

Public private partnerships and the private finance initiative

Third, there are hybrid public-private models, like the private finance initiative (PFI) and public private partnerships (PPPs). In this case the state commissions the project, the private sector provides the capital investment to fund the asset, designs, builds and operates the asset (a new school or hospital, for example) and receives income from the state for the lifetime of that asset – generally around 30 years. While the first PFI contracts were awarded by the 1992–97 Conservative government, Labour made much more extensive use of these arrangements, securing a big programme of public investment without having to engage in additional borrowing. In principle, the construction risk (cost overruns) and the investment risk were all borne by the private sector, insulating the government from responsibility for these matters and reducing the level of borrowing on the balance sheet. In practice, however, the government still shouldered most of the risks. When the PPP for the tube collapsed in 2010, responsibility reverted to London Underground Limited. The same is true for those PFI contracts affected by the collapse of Carillion in January 2018. Whether the remaining PFI deals represent good value for money is a matter of empirical evidence which, at the time of writing, suggests that more conventional methods of financing would have produced better value for money for the taxpayer. Government can always borrow more cheaply than the private sector and using conventional methods of government borrowing would not have required either the complex contracts or significant payments to private consortia over a 30-year period.

It ought to be a matter of concern for social democrats that so many of these policy mistakes happened on Labour's watch. Given historical experience and Labour's reputation for profligacy, one cannot decry the 1997–2010 government's desire to demonstrate that it was 'prudent'. But the use of incredibly complicated mechanisms to fund the construction of public assets looks, with the benefit of hindsight, to have been tactically astute in the short term (nobody can deny that lots of secondary schools and hospitals were built as a result) and strategically catastrophic in the long term. Of course, defenders of the model will say that the collapse of Carillion was a consequence of the downward pressure on financing applied by a Conservative government committed to austerity (PFI consortia were expected to do more for a reduced revenue stream) but that still cannot explain the collapse of the PPP on London Underground or the 'refinancing' of earlier PFI deals, which reduced the borrowing costs of the private sector without any commensurate reductions in the charges to government. The case for a new approach is compelling.

Ends and means

Perhaps we should go further and say that New Labour fell into an ideological trap as a result of a failure to think through what makes public services different from the goods and services available in private markets. To begin with, it seemed that the 1997–2010 government was adopting a pragmatic or agnostic approach, exemplified by the mantra "what matters is what works", suggesting that whether or not a market or private sector involvement was warranted would depend on the evidence at the time. But towards the end of his period as prime minister, Tony Blair was more than comfortable making statements like this:

> In the business world, adjustment to change comes through the market. You adapt or you go out of business. In the public services, the profit and loss accountability does not exist, at least in anything like the same way.[4]

This observation could be read as little more than a statement of fact; public services are not in the business of making profits. But in the context of Blair's broader argument, the implication is clear: in the absence of market pressures public services are less adaptable and less accountable to consumers than their private sector counterparts. Perhaps this is best viewed as a category error, a mistake about what makes public services different and distinctive. In the words of Professor Mark Moore, a public management theorist at the Kennedy School of Government:

> *[W]e should evaluate the efforts of public sector managers not in the economic marketplace of individual consumers but in the political marketplace of citizens and the collective decisions of representative democratic institutions* (Moore 1995).

Gordon Brown offered a slightly different assessment in 2003, referring specifically to the NHS, arguing that markets in healthcare have significant disadvantages. He suggested that the price mechanism cannot work in the provision of health services, the consumer is not sovereign, there is a potential abuse of monopoly power, it is hard to write and enforce contracts, it is difficult if not impossible to let a hospital go bust, and suppliers can manipulate the market to create or induce demand. In other words, all the conditions are present to diagnose a market failure, leading to the conclusion that the government has an obligation to intervene. Nonetheless, he expressed strong commitment to the belief that the NHS cannot be a wholly centralised service, that contestability between public and private providers is a permanent feature of the landscape, and that consumer choice, within the limits of the analysis, remains a relevant consideration (Brown 2003).

One might say that the then chancellor was using conventional economic arguments ("market failure") to secure progressive ends. But it is reasonable to ask whether it was market failure that inspired the post-1945 Labour government to create the NHS. More important, perhaps, was a commitment to the belief that healthcare, free at the point of need, is a citizenship good, which should be entirely unrelated to the ability to pay. By arguing in such conventional terms both Gordon Brown and Tony Blair were devaluing the notion of citizenship and the principle that democratic accountability imposes disciplines on public managers that are just as rigorous as market mechanisms.

Arguably, events took this course because, as a result of persistent election defeats, Labour failed to develop its own, equally persuasive, approach to public services as an alternative to the market fundamentalist delusions of Thatcherism.[5] It would be wrong to condemn the Blair government entirely for this, but policy always reverts to the mean or the pre-existing status quo unless civil servants are given a clear signal that something fundamental needs to change. Leading figures in New Labour therefore bear a heavy responsibility for not thinking deeply enough about the challenges they faced and for executing rapid U-turns that restored the direction of policy that had prevailed under Conservative administrations. At the beginning of Labour's time in office, for example, the internal market in the NHS was abolished; by the end of the government's life, on the other hand, the goal was to create quasi-markets in both health and education. The absence of a compelling narrative about public services was another failure of social democratic modernisation, which left the field open to Jeremy Corbyn's unsophisticated hostility to all forms of 'privatisation'.

A useful place to start, perhaps, is an open conversation about the limits of the public and the private sectors. Again, I am not suggesting that there is a right answer to this question that can stand for all time; circumstances change, boundaries shift, trade-offs have to be made. Nonetheless, it is important to have a consensus on these questions before Labour returns to government, not least to avoid disappointment or unnecessary disputes in the parliamentary Labour party.

Michael Sandel in *What Money Can't Buy* argues that subjecting a particular good to market processes can change the *nature* of that good; its production and distribution may have been governed by non-market norms, but now they are subject to market disciplines, the fixing of prices through a competitive process, with the objective of producing a profit for the provider (Sandel 2012). If we take healthcare as an obvious example, patients would be justifiably worried if clinicians were principally motivated by the desire to maximise either their personal wealth or shareholder value for a private business. Doctors have professional obligations to their patients, they want to make people well again and they have a relationship of trust with people in their care. To assert that this relationship is no different from a customer paying for their goods at the supermarket checkout is to make a serious mistake indeed.

The same might be said for education, from primary schools to universities, where respect for learning and pastoral care outweigh any considerations of profit and loss. Or for the child protection services of local authorities, where the suggestion that profits might be made from the misfortunes of vulnerable children will lead many of us to feel more than a little uneasy. Of course teachers, doctors and social workers want to be rewarded fairly (as do we all) but their motivations are *intrinsic* rather than *extrinsic*; they are professionals, take pride in what they do and will, quite rightly, resist the notion that their performance can be improved through payment by results or other financial incentives.

It could be said that these are easy cases, where the notion of the public service ethos can be readily understood. But public services cover a wide range of activities, from complex neurosurgery to refuse collection, and devising a set of principles applicable to all these activities is a supremely difficult task. It is almost certainly the case that professionals operating in private markets are activated by intrinsic motivations. Lawyers have an obligation to do the best they can for their clients; architects want their buildings to be enjoyed by the people who live and work in them; those employed in the creative industries want to be respected for the quality of their art, not simply the revenue it generates. In other words, non-market norms play a role in most human activity. We can see this in the work of Adam Smith too who, despite being misinterpreted as a prophet of self-interested, wealth-maximising behaviour, also emphasised the importance of "sympathy" as a motivation that makes a civilised society possible (Smith 1759). To quote Gordon Brown again, this time with approbation, "markets need morals"; if the only objective is to maximise wealth then it is doubtful whether any market could work at all.

Democracy, accountability, participation

Beyond the inevitably contested public-private boundary lies a wider problem. Just how should the state, in all its manifestations, relate to citizens? What does it mean, in practice, to say that democracy and accountability are more powerful instruments for the delivery of quality and value for money than a straightforward application of market norms? Governments of differing hues have talked about the importance of citizen or service user involvement. Support for consultation, of various kinds, appears to be a matter of political consensus. But there are plenty of experiences to prove that the reverse may be equally true. The default setting in many cases is that politicians decide on a certain course of action, public servants are instructed to execute that decision and consultation comes as an afterthought.

The controversy about housing policy in the north London borough of Haringey is a case in point, where the council's preferred solution – a long-term partnership with a private consortium to develop the social housing stock and other public assets – was opposed by council tenants and by the Momentum faction in the local Labour party. It is at least arguable that a more open and transparent process, where tenants and other stakeholders were consulted on various options *before* any decisions were taken, would have led to a different arrangement and a better outcome.[6] The same might be said for consultation on traffic-calming arrangements in a locality, changes to recycling policies or, more controversially, the reconfiguration of NHS services. Politics is about choices and, under current arrangements, the nature of those choices is often concealed from the electorate, or at least not explained with an adequate degree of respect for the intelligence of the voter. Of course, we live in a representative democracy, most citizens are not and do not wish to be either politicians or policy wonks, and ultimately choices must be made by elected representatives who can be held responsible for their decisions. More openness and transparency does not mean passing the buck back to the electorate, but it does mean treating voters with respect and demonstrating that politicians can be both attentive and responsive to public concerns.

THE CAPACITY OF THE STATE AND A NEW CONSTITUTIONAL SETTLEMENT?

A critical element of the argument presented in this volume is that the state has an important role to play in protecting people in conditions of rapid change, building capabilities to allow people to find solid ground on which to stand in a very different world and creating national and regional institutions to ensure that prosperity is distributed more widely than has been the case in the last three decades. All of this depends on the state having the capabilities it needs to develop and execute policy. Devising a shiny new initiative in Whitehall is one thing, making it a reality in Rotherham or Grimsby quite another.

Labour will inherit a weakened policymaking machine, denuded of expertise and resources. Local government will be struggling to cope with more than a decade of cuts. And the city-region mayors, while the novelty of their office may have inspired some optimism, will be under pressure to deliver the ambitious goals they have set. An important early action of a newly elected Labour government must be to undertake a review of the capacities of the state and decide, given other manifesto priorities, how the machinery of government can be rebuilt so that it is efficient, responsive and effective.

These practical difficulties are compounded by a more serious problem: the UK's constitutional settlement between the regions and the nations is a mess and in urgent need of repair. Scottish nationalism has not disappeared and another independence referendum is in prospect if the UK fails to secure the softest of soft Brexits. "English votes for English laws" is now a reality, making Scottish MPs second-class citizens in the House of Commons. Regional government in England is a patchwork; there is some devolution to the metro mayors but most significant policies remain the exclusive responsibility of Whitehall. There may not yet be a clamour for new institutions of regional government, but it is at least arguable that public opinion is tending in that direction, partly in response to the failure of national policies to regenerate the left-behind communities of the Midlands and the north.

The Conservative party depends on English votes. Scotland does not matter much to them, despite the modest revival in Conservative fortunes in the 2017 general election, largely attributable to Ruth Davidson's efforts to distance herself from Theresa May's campaign. Some Conservatives are also willing to risk a return to violence in Northern Ireland, deliberately undermining the Good Friday agreement, in the pursuit of a hard Brexit that disentangles the whole of the UK from the single market and the customs union.

From one standpoint Labour is not only the most credible unionist party remaining, but the only major party that is united in looking for a practical solution to the border question on the island of Ireland. Whether by default or by design, Labour will have no alternative but to address the constitutional question well before the 2022 election. Some sceptics may say that this is a foolish statement; the electorate are never enthused by arcane constitutional niceties, the devolution settlement is in place and Scottish nationalism can be seen off by a Corbyn-friendly Scottish Labour party. There is no need to kick the hornets' nest, particularly when a progressive government has other priorities.

Certainly, this argument is worthy of consideration, but it does seem more than a little complacent. How, for example, is Labour to engineer a political recovery in Scotland, which is essential for a general election victory, if it has no response to the SNP's claim that independence is the only progressive option in a post-Brexit world, allowing Scotland to remain in the EU? How can the Labour coalition be rebuilt if nothing is done to construct new institutions that are focused on reviving the prosperity of disadvantaged regions? Moreover, there is an equally strong case for saying that real regional devolution, going beyond the creation of the metro mayors, is necessary to reunite the country. Bringing politics closer to the people can restore faith in the democratic process, by making it more relevant to immediate concerns. Labour has to prove that it is committed to doing politics differently and that means developing a coherent federal structure for the governance of the UK.

Again, a sceptic will say that these measures will make the problem worse not better, encouraging people to look inwards not outwards and abandoning the idea of national standards in the NHS and education. An obvious response is that devolution does not necessarily have these effects; it depends on which powers are devolved, the extent of revenue-raising at the regional or local level and the relationship with national policies. Moreover, if one looks at outcomes, then, despite the existence of national policies developed in Whitehall, not all regions are equally prosperous, or healthy, or well educated. Simply driving everything from the centre has not delivered the same outcomes in different parts of the country.

BRITAIN IN EUROPE AND THE WORLD

At the heart of progressive politics is the belief that global problems require global solutions, that dialogue is better than conflict and that an array of international institutions is essential to support those objectives. It is for this reason that social democrats are against the turning inwards associated with nationalism. Support for Brexit, scepticism about the value of defence and security co-operation and a 'beggar thy neighbour' approach to trade policy are all inconsistent with the values of the left. In the past the UK has been at the forefront of arguing for the establishment of international labour standards, played an especially important role in reducing the debt burden of developing nations and led the response of the leading industrial nations to the global financial crisis. While no longer a power of global importance, the UK still has a good deal of influence and it should be the goal of a Labour government to ensure that this influence is used for progressive ends.

Brexit

The most obvious foreign policy challenge facing the UK is dealing with the consequences of Brexit. At the time of writing (February 2018), the UK government had yet to outline the nature of the relationship it is seeking with the EU, had failed to explain how the question of the border on the island of Ireland is to be resolved and had fixed a series of red lines that made it difficult to see how an orderly transition could take place, culminating in the UK leaving the customs union and the single market.

Offering anything useful beyond generalities on the subject is difficult because events are moving so fast. What is undeniable, however, is that Labour cannot continue to fudge the question of the UK's continuing relationship with the EU. In the short term the issues are principally about tactical manoeuvres in the House of Commons to embarrass the government and, potentially, minimise the consequences of the UK crashing out of the EU without either a transitional deal or any clarity about the arrangements to be applied in a post-Brexit world. But that means too that Labour must be clearer about its own objectives.

Arguing for a 'jobs first Brexit' is almost as meaningless as arguing for a 'red, white and blue Brexit'. All the economic evidence points to a clear conclusion: the UK will be worse off after leaving the largest free trade area in the world. If Labour wants to implement a programme of economic and social regeneration then it needs to have policy instruments available to sustain full employment, ensure that economic growth continues and raise the taxes needed to fund public expenditure. Uncertainty about the shape of the post-Brexit world puts these ambitions in jeopardy. Life outside the EU will be cold, hostile and lonely. To believe anything else is to endorse the fantasies of the extreme Brexiteers. Neil Kinnock was right to say that stopping Brexit is the best route to saving the NHS.

Recent announcements suggest that major corporations are considering a complete exit from the UK or at least a scaling back of their operations. If the City of London has no access to the EU's markets under the so-called passporting arrangements, then the UK's comparative advantage in the finance sector will be profoundly damaged[7]. A good deal of economic harm has been done already, with a significant devaluation of sterling leading to increases in import prices and the re-emergence of inflation as a concern for the Bank of England. Once the UK has left the EU it is reasonable to believe that pressure on the currency will intensify, interest rates will rise and growth will fall.

Parliament will have the opportunity to vote on the withdrawal agreement negotiated by Theresa May before the UK finally leaves the EU. At which point Labour will have to decide whether to support or oppose that settlement. Ultimately, Jeremy Corbyn and his colleagues must make a judgement about whether leaving the EU is genuinely in the national interest.

For the time being, most politicians across the political spectrum have to express support for the implementation of the referendum result; a swift review of speeches delivered by leading figures in government and opposition suggest that Brexit is an unstoppable juggernaut. But the whole point about a democracy is that no decision is fixed for all time. As Keynes said, "when the facts change I change my mind". There can be little doubt that the facts have now changed or, more accurately, that the practical implications of leaving the EU are much clearer than was the case in June 2016.

At some point in the next year Labour will be faced with a stark choice: either collaborate in the unfolding disaster that is Brexit or oppose the process completely and be bold in making the case that the UK should, despite the referendum result, remain in the EU. Arguably, Keir Starmer's 'six tests' which Theresa May's Brexit deal must pass before it secures Labour's support simply cannot be met, since all the possible options are inferior to the status quo and cannot deliver the 'exact same benefits' that the UK enjoys today. Whether the party will have the courage to make this case is uncertain, but a failure to be honest with the electorate now will simply postpone the day of reckoning until after the 2022 general election.

Imagine, for example, that Brexit takes place in 2019 with no solution to the Irish border question and a rejection of membership of the customs union and the single market. If Labour wins in 2022 it will confront a series of questions that cannot be avoided. Should the UK seek to rejoin the customs union and the single market? Is it appropriate for the UK to seek the same status as Norway? Will a Labour government accept the jurisdiction of the European court of justice and the four freedoms of the EU (free movement for goods, services, capital and people)? Should the UK seek some safeguards on the free movement of people to supplement those already provided by the EU treaties? Is this a red line for a future negotiation with the EU, or will a Labour government concede that, on balance, acceptance of the four freedoms is a reasonable price for market access?

I am cognisant of the fact that the argument in the previous paragraphs puts me out of step with many people in Labour's mainstream. But no progressive party in the UK can be an anti-European party, even if many or even most social democrats believe that the EU needs fundamental reform. It is inconceivable, for example, that any trade agreement the UK reaches with another country will be superior to the market access guaranteed by EU membership. Nor is it plausible to believe that the UK, acting alone, can achieve a more favourable agreement with the US, India or China than could be achieved through the EU. Every country expects a quid pro quo for access to their markets and the relative size of the countries concerned determines negotiating clout. The British people should be prepared for a series of lop-sided arrangements that do less than expected to compensate for the UK's decision to stand alone. Corbyn and McDonnell, if they are serious about delivering their programme and protecting their national interest, must abandon their instinctive Euroscepticism and embrace the case for the UK's continued membership of the single market as well as the customs union. All other options will leave Labour in a position where it can only disappoint in government, as the bright hopes of economic and social regeneration are dimmed by the long shadow of Brexit.

Defence and security

Since 1945 all Labour governments have been committed to the notion of collective security in Europe. Nato membership has, until recently, been endorsed by all Labour leaders as necessary for the protection of the national interest. This was the case even when the party was committed to unilateral nuclear disarmament. The 1983 manifesto may have called for the UK to abandon the deterrent, but it would have still left the country sheltering under the US' nuclear umbrella.

Denis Healey often bemoaned the absence of a Labour foreign policy culture, implying that not enough people had thought seriously or realistically enough about how a Labour government should behave. On the left there was (and remains) a romantic attachment to national liberation struggles, anti-imperialism and a profound hostility to the US. On much of a the right of the party, the standard position has been a crude Atlanticism, allied with anti-communism during the cold war, exemplified by Nato membership and defence and security co-operation with the US. One can see why profound disagreements might arise between these two incompatible views of the world.

But Healey's point still stands. Both approaches are a little unreflective and indicate that, beyond a small number of unilateralist enthusiasts or those concerned about the fate of developing nations, foreign and defence policy has been towards the bottom of the list of Labour activists' priorities. If we want to understand the UK's disastrous joint intervention with the US in Iraq, for example, we need do no more than refer to the default setting of crude Atlanticism.

Whatever we may think of Blair's moral arguments for the removal of Saddam Hussein, one cannot deny that staying close to the Americans was an important motivation. Arguably, this desire also blinded the prime minister to the likely consequences of military intervention – Arabists in the Foreign Office understood that regime change in Iraq was likely to destabilise the Middle East as a whole - and we are still living with the aftershocks today. Other Labour prime ministers have managed the transatlantic relationship with rather more independence of mind. Harold Wilson, for example, resisted Lyndon Johnson's attempts to secure British participation in the Vietnam war, not because he thought a significant minority of the parliamentary Labour party would be opposed to that course of action, but because he believed that course of action to be a strategic mistake.[8]

There is a strong case for saying that both conventional stances, default Atlanticism and romantic anti-imperialism, no longer provide any useful guidance to the development and execution of foreign policy, if they ever did. In a world where the US can no longer be viewed as a reliable partner, with a more aggressive Russia and new powers like China emerging on the global stage, it is clear that Atlanticism has outlived its usefulness. Equally, the anti-imperialist stance that formed Jeremy Corbyn's politics has even less to say about these emerging foreign policy challenges.

A natural conclusion is that there must be greater defence co-operation in Europe, not through Nato but through the EU. Quite how this can be reconciled with Brexit, despite Theresa May's commitment to a "deep and special partnership" remains an open question, creating an opportunity for Labour to make the case that the Tories are putting national security at risk.

The biggest mistake Labour could make in the next four years, however, would be to fall into the trap of an arid discussion about whether the UK should, or should not, retain a nuclear deterrent. Of course, the context has changed since the election of Donald Trump. It had been assumed, hitherto, that any replacement for the Trident programme would depend on close co-operation with the US – the

UK would build the submarines and the warheads, the US would provide the missile delivery system. That option looks much less attractive when the Oval Office is occupied by a capricious individual who announces major foreign policy decisions by tweet.

On the other hand, the case for maintaining some nuclear capacity is strong, not just because US intentions are uncertain, but because a retreat by the US from Europe and unilateral disarmament by the UK will leave France and Russia as the only nuclear-armed states on the continent. As David Clark has pointed out, Vladimir Putin is quite content to use the possession of nuclear weapons as an instrument to coerce other nations to take actions they would otherwise resist (Clark 2015). For the time being, the UK must remain a nuclear-capable state.

Perhaps what Labour needs on foreign, defence and security policy is an open discussion that moves beyond the standard arguments of left and right. A judicious assessment of the risks must be matched by a realistic appreciation of the UK's role in the world and in Europe, with much greater clarity about where defence and security sit in the scale of Labour's priorities. The difficulties should not be underestimated and, despite the desire of many on the left for an ethical foreign policy, Robin Cook's experience in government proves that even the best intentions are an incomplete guide when confronted with the realpolitik of dealing with somewhat unsavoury regimes. If the world really is in a state of flux then social democrats need to be flexible in their response. Cold war ideological preconceptions are of no use whatsoever. Nonetheless, social democrats need to be able to convince the electorate that they can keep the nation safe. A failure to do so is a guaranteed recipe for defeat.

THE CHALLENGE TO DEMOCRACY

What I have sought to do in this final chapter is address *some* of the issues that Labour must address if it is to build a sustainable electoral coalition that can secure victory in 2022 and provide a sound foundation for a successful reforming government. I make no claim to comprehensiveness. Nor am I suggesting that every proposal presented here is right or the only route forward for social democracy. The intention throughout this volume has been to provoke a conversation between people with shared values, not present a detailed programme as the only route to political success.

At the close of Chapter 1 I made brief reference to the challenges facing most of the developed democracies in the richest parts of the world, recording declining faith in the political mainstream and the rise of populism. At the heart of the problem is a disjunction between the theoretical foundations of our institutions and the operation of democracy in practice. In principle, we all count for one and no more than one when the balance of opinion is weighed; in practice some individuals and interest groups enjoy disproportionate access to power.

There is a school of thought on the political right that to expect more public engagement than we have today is absurd. People are rational in believing that they have limited practical influence on any decision between elections, and determinedly refusing to take an interest in politics does no more than reflect reality. From this standpoint it is the normal condition of democracy to have a moderately disconnected and disaffected electorate. By taking such a cynical view, however, one can easily become complacent and fail to notice serious challenges to the sustainability of our institutions. My case, to the contrary, is that a deliberate effort has to be made to restore public trust and that means social democrats have to consider how to do politics differently.

For the Corbynistas, the solution is to transform Labour into a social movement, with hundreds of thousands of party members making the case on the doorstep. A large body of politically motivated people can help to sustain Labour in government by defending the achievements of 'socialism' in everyday discussions with their friends, neighbours and colleagues, and by campaigning continuously to shift the political centre of gravity in a leftwards direction. In practice, this model may be just as unrealistic as what Stephen

Pinker calls the "civics class" approach to democracy, where well-informed citizens participate in deliberative discussions to ensure the good governance of the *polis* (Pinker 2018).[9]

The same may be true of the Labour party's democracy review, which is supposedly about empowering members in the development of policy, suggesting that Labour's programme should be the outcome of a process with extensive member participation. From this standpoint every member becomes a policy expert, apparently with well-developed views on the correct orientation of macroeconomic policy, the reconstruction of the welfare state or defence and foreign policy. Perhaps the biggest difficulty here is that it neglects the importance of prioritisation and the unavoidable reality that resources are constrained.[10] Party members certainly ought to be able to influence the general direction that Labour takes and can act as an ideological compass if the leadership is straying too far from Labour's core values. But Labour members will struggle if they are asked to make complex choices and trade-offs; they are not experts in policy design and execution and in many cases have no wish to be. If every member really were a committed policy wonk, we might legitimately wonder how anything would ever get done – because wonks, more than anything else, love sitting in seminar rooms and talking.[11]

What Labour and other social democratic parties need, perhaps, is a more sophisticated understanding between ordinary members and political leaders. Just what rights do you have as a party member? What influence is it reasonable to expect over policy? And how can policy be entirely member-led when the Labour party in particular is composed of individual members, affiliated trade unions and socialist societies?[12] The risk is clear: a return to the resolutionary socialism of Labour party conferences of the past, with opaque composite motions, cobbled together from contradictory propositions leaving the hard work of policy development to the front bench and the policy sub-committees of the national executive. There is a strong case for saying that, constitutionally, Labour's policymaking process already allows for a more effective deliberative exercise.

The challenge is to make these institutions (the policy commissions and the National Policy Forum) work in the new environment of a larger membership, giving serious consideration to additional mechanisms that allow for some element of wider participation. My fear, however, is that the democracy review will, in practice, lead to an outcome where, if anything, policy development is restricted to a small group in the leader's office complemented by some insiders on the front bench. This will not be a superior system and it will certainly not demonstrate Labour's willingness to do politics differently.

Part of the answer may be a change in political style, away from the professionally presented centrism of the New Labour years, to something that is more open, honest and modest. Modesty in this context could be equally described as humility – a recognition that politicians do not know everything, have to cope with the unexpected and have to be honest when they have got something wrong. Part of the problem today, perhaps, is that no politician can ever admit to a mistake. Invariably, a trial by media follows, with the public being given the message: 'look, they don't know what they are doing, you can't trust them'.

Jeremy Corbyn's great advantage is that he is an example of 'anti-style', which can be readily mistaken for authenticity. Being really authentic, however, means exposing ones frailties as well as one's strengths and demonstrating that ambitious objectives are reflected by the effectiveness of policy implementation. To that extent, the Corbynistas could easily experience the same syndrome as New Labour, where rhetorical reach is beyond the government's policy grasp. Grand new initiatives are announced but the practical reality falls short. Modesty demands the avoidance of extravagant claims, new dawns or shining cities on the hill.

That a change in style is needed is reflected in the retreat of social democracy across Europe. Although not every party went through the same transformation as New Labour, most leading figures on the centre left adopted similar strategies in responding to the challenge of winning votes from a largely uninterested electorate. Everybody has, to a greater or lesser extent, embraced the idea of politics as a product and of parties as brands. Recent election results show this political model failing *everywhere,* including the UK.

Social democrats are rationalists. We believe that problems can be solved through the intelligent intervention of government, using evidence to develop policies that have a decent chance of delivering their promise and by being willing to move on to another experiment if it appears that a particular instrument is not working as expected. We also believe that politics demands giving all views a fair hearing. Silencing our opponents is not our aim; every citizen is entitled to respect and nobody is a traitor, a wrecker or a saboteur just because they hold views not congruent with our own. In other words, social democrats are defenders of the values of the Enlightenment and of civility in politics. Expressed in these terms, it is very easy for social democracy to sound as if it is out of step with the times.

Because, make no mistake, civility and politics make uneasy bed-fellows today. Donald Trump, far-right populists in Europe and the trolling denizens of social media are living, breathing examples of the coarsening of political discourse. To paraphrase Amartya Sen, this is where the nastiness has crept in. And the phenomenon is not just restricted to the right. The *ad hominem* attacks on Labour MPs by over-enthusiastic Corbynistas are from the same stable, as are the outpourings from websites like The Skwawkbox, Novara Media and The Canary. It could be argued that these phenomena are equal and opposite reactions to the awfulness of the right; in such conditions the left has no alternative but to fight fire with fire. But the difficulty with this stance is that it imposes no boundaries on acceptable behaviour, it is an anarchic world where opinion is everything, passion trumps reason and facts do not matter. A sceptic will say that the genie has been released and there is nothing to be done, but it is hard to see how progress can be made unless part of Labour's mission (shared with social democrats across Europe) is to restore civility and reason to politics.

Central to the case made here is the belief that social democracy represents the best in us. It seeks to give practical effect to formal rights, to enlarge the sphere of freedom of all citizens by giving them the capabilities they need to choose lives they have reason to value. A strong welfare state, efficient and effective public services and a robust system of economic democracy enable people to go out into the world, have adventures and enjoy everything that life has to offer. What may look like prosaic and bureaucratic models can enhance the human experience. The goal is to make capitalism work for everybody, to create inclusive prosperity, to eliminate poverty, discrimination and low pay by using the power of the state, through collective action, to forge a society where equal citizenship is guaranteed.

These desirable outcomes cannot be delivered by some illusory politics of transformation, by uprooting all existing institutions and replacing them with who knows what. Social democrats do not intend to change *everything,* but we are devoted to equal citizenship and social justice; eliminating present evils is central to the mission. Part of our story has been about the profound human need for stability, for security, for solid ground on which to stand when the world is in flux. Gunter Grass once suggested the purpose of social democracy is to achieve "progress in stasis" – if we want to achieve change then we have to ensure that some things stay the same, otherwise people will revolt against the upheaval (Grass 1972)[13]. He also compared social democracy to a snail, which was meant as a compliment; slow moving, resilient, determined and with a clear sense of direction. Perhaps the greatest social democratic virtue, above all others, is patience.

NOTES

CHAPTER 1

1. Witness, for example, the changing stance of Larry Summers, former US Treasury Secretary. An architect of financial market deregulation in the 1990s, Summers is now an enthusiast for higher minimum wages, stronger trade unions, industrial democracy and extensive public investment to build the productive potential of the economy (Center for American Progress 2015).

2. Until the emergence of Jeremy Corbyn and Bernie Sanders, of course, at which point more full-throated denunciation became the order of the day.

3. Although the increase in agricultural productivity in the UK in the eighteenth and nineteenth centuries disrupted rural life and spurred the movement from country to town. There were more jobs at better wages in the factory system, even if the quality of living and working conditions had deteriorated.

4. Schumpeter believed, with regret, that some form of "socialism" was inevitable because citizens in democracies would reject as intolerable the insecurity associated with creative destruction (Schumpeter 1943).

5. Which is not to deny of, course, that there are many households in Manchester today living in accommodation below a decent standard. Nor am I denying than many households struggle to make ends meet.

6. The first indication of the credit crunch in August 2007 came when French bank BNP Paribas told investors that they would be unable to withdraw their investments from two funds because of a "complete collapse of liquidity in the market".

7. In his memoir, *The Road to Nab End*, William Woodruff recalls the earlier decline of the cotton industry in Blackburn in the 1920s and 1930s. This was a story about investment, technology and creative destruction. Nobody talked about globalisation at the time, although the mill workers were concerned about "unfair competition" from lower cost producers.

8. The National Economic Development Council (NEDC), bringing together government, trade unions and employers, was established by Harold Macmillan's Conservative government in 1962 – and abolished by John Major's Conservative government in 1992.

9. Exemplified by the Ford sewing machinists' strike of 1968, which led directly to the Equal Pay Act 1970.

CHAPTER 2

1. Some readers were obviously alienated. Bernstein was subjected to merciless attacks by orthodox Marxists and by those of a more radical temper, like Rosa Luxemburg (Wright 1986).

2. This is just as much as lesson for ideologues on the right as on the left. Thatcherism failed because it was unbendingly ideological in its ambition to remake society.

3. In simpler language, Lenin, Trotsky, Stalin and Mao were all wrong.

4. Of course, many of Jeremy Corbyn's closest associates are not democratic socialists at all, drawing their inspiration from Lenin and Stalin rather than the richer, more liberal tradition found in western Europe (including some variants of western Marxism).

5. I should acknowledge a debt here to Raymond Plant's *Equality, Markets and the State* (Plant 1984). Much of this section has been profoundly influenced by Lord Plant's ideas. I bear full responsibility for the interpretation.

6. It may seem a little archaic, but I find laissez-faire a more illuminating descriptor than neo-liberalism, which is used all too frequently as a catch-all to embrace everything people on the left find offensive.

7. See, for example, the criminalisation of homosexuality until the Sexual Offences Act 1967.

8. Berlin's target is not just Marxism, but the philosophy of Hegel and the German Idealists. Bertrand Russell was especially rude about Hegel in *A History of Western Philosophy* (1945), suggesting that, for Hegel, the ideal or "the absolute" was revealed (almost) in an individual's willingness to comply with the diktats of the Prussian state.

9. Gordon Brown talks about "fair outcomes" of course, but one wonders whether this idea can be made consistent with a plausible conception of equality of opportunity.

10. This is not to criticise the efforts of Alan Milburn's Social Mobility Commission, which produced a huge quantity of compelling research documenting the impact of inequality on life chances. It might, more appropriately, have been described as an Inequality Commission.

11. Although the Bennite position in the 1980s was that only members of constituency general management committees should be able to participate in the reselection process – the majority of party members were excluded. Democracy obviously had limits.

12. Arguably, Britain was a notably irreligious society from the middle of the nineteenth century onwards, at which point the majority of the population had abandoned church attendance, even if they still professed some form of religious belief (Cannadine 2017).

CHAPTER 3

1. Which meant too that Labour never had a persuasive account of the relationship between anti-inflation policies and the free collective bargaining treasured by trade unions. The government may have wanted to plan incomes, but the unions were always resistant.

2. The study was based on a relatively small sample of workers, which was then grossed up to generate the effects across the whole labour market of 31 million people.

3. The TUC's analysis shows that median earnings for ZHC workers are around 60% of the median for the working population as a whole.

4. Which means that workers with ZHCs, although relatively few in number, are more than *twice* as likely to be low paid as the rest of the working population, where one in five is low paid.

5. The joint paper produced by Tony Blair and Gerhard Schröder was quite explicit on this point. See *Die Neue Mitte-The Third Way* (1998*).* "*The labour market needs a low wage sector in order to make low skill jobs available. The tax and benefits system can replenish low incomes from employment and at the same time save on support payments for the unemployed".*

6. Although the German system is not incorruptible, as the Volkswagen diesel emissions scandal has proved.

7. As with the wages councils, it would be sensible for these bodies to include some independent members to encourage consensus and break any deadlock between the employer and worker representatives.

CHAPTER 4

1. At the beginning of the nineteenth century, water services were largely in private hands. A process of creeping nationalisation had, by the beginning of the twentieth century, placed most water utilities in municipal ownership, and then following the reforms of the 1945–1951 Labour government, in the hands of Regional Water Authorities.

2. Perhaps the Air New Zealand case is better seen as an example of Crosland's notion of competitive public enterprise – the airline is now a global leader and operates in a highly competitive international market. The recently elected Labour government has no intention of changing the airline's ownership structure.

3. Which is precisely what Theresa May's government is doing, taking a leaf from Labour's 2015 manifesto and imposing a price cap on energy tariffs.

4. Rt Hon Tony Blair MP, speech on public service reform, 6 June 2006.

5. Although this is a little unfair to Margaret Thatcher, since most of the market reforms to the NHS were introduced after she left office. Understanding the public commitment to the health service, she was wary of bold moves and was more pragmatic than most of her successors.

6. Richard Sennett offers a compelling account of more deliberative models of governance, with extensive community *and* expert involvement in *Building and Dwelling* (2018).

7. Whatever our views of the financial sector, a major exodus from the City will have a depressive effect on government revenues, making it more difficult for Labour to deliver an ambitious programme.

8. The UK had significant military assets in south-east Asia until the end of the Vietnam War, including a large naval base in Singapore. In 1968 Wilson and Healey took the decision gradually to withdraw these forces, a process completed in 1976. The decision to stay out of Vietnam certainly created transatlantic tensions, but nobody could deny that Wilson and Healey (then defence secretary) were committed to the western alliance.

9. Even the classical models of democracy produced somewhat troubling results – after all it was a democratic decision by an Athenian jury to condemn Socrates to death.

10. Labour's 1983 manifesto gives us a flavour of what a 'member-led' programme might deliver – either a dog's breakfast or the longest suicide note in history.

11. Mea culpa.

12. Other social democratic parties, lacking Labour's confederal structure, may find it easier to answer this question.

13. This sounds a lot like Blue Labour, confirming my earlier observation that Glasman's version of Labour's future is German social democracy with some English nationalist seasoning. Grass' *From the Diary of a Snail* is a fictionalised account of the story of the Jews of Danzig and a factual account of his participation in Willi Brandt's successful campaign in the German federal election of 1969.

BIBLIOGRAPHY

Akerlof, George (1970), The Market for Lemons: Quality Uncertainty and the Market Process, Quarterly Journal of Economics 84(3), MIT Press.

Arntz, Melanie et al. (2016), The Risks of Automation for Jobs in OECD Countries: A Comparative Analysis, OECD Social, Employment and Migration Working Papers No 189, Organisation for Economic Co-operation and Development.

Bailey, Jess et al. (2011), Painful Separation: An International Study of the Weakening Relationship between Economic Growth and the Pay of Ordinary Workers, Resolution Foundation/Commission on Living Standards.

Berg, Andrew and Ostry, Jonathan (2011), Inequality and Unsustainable Growth: Two Sides of the Same Coin? IMF Staff Discussion Note, SDN/11/08, International Monetary Fund.

Berlin, Isaiah (1969), Four Essays on Liberty, Oxford University Press.

Bernstein, Eduard (1899), Evolutionary Socialism, Shocken Books, 2nd edition 1963.

Berriman, Richard and Hawksworth, John (2017), Will Robots Steal Our Jobs? The Potential Impact of Automation on the UK and Other Major Economies, PwC.

Brinkley, Ian (2016), In Search of the Gig Economy, The Work Foundation.

Brinkley, Ian (2016), Why the Robots Are Not Coming for Your Job, The Work Foundation.

Brown, Gordon (2003), A New Agenda for Prosperity and Reform, SMF Lecture, February 2003.

Brown, Gordon (2006), Introduction to The Future of Socialism, 50th anniversary edition, Constable.

Budd, John (2004), Employment with A Human Face, Cornell University Press.

Brynjolfsson, Erik and McAfee, Andrew (2014), The Second Machine Age: Work, Progress and Prosperity in a Time of Brilliant Technologies, W.W. Norton.

Bryson, Alex and Forth, John (2016), The Added Value of Unions, Trades Union Congress.

Cannadine, David (2017), Victorious Century: The United Kingdom 1800–1906, Allen Lane.

Clark, David (2015), Open to the World: How the Left's Foreign Policy Can Face the Future, The Fabian Society.

Coats, David (2009), Advancing Opportunity: The Future of Good Work, The Smith Institute.

Coats, David (2013), Just Deserts?, The Smith Institute.

Commission on Inclusive Prosperity (2015), Report of the Commission on Inclusive Prosperity, Center for American Progress.

Commission on Living Standards (2012), Gaining From Growth: Final Report of the Commission on Living Standards, Resolution Foundation.

Corlett, Adam et al. (2017), The Living Standards Audit, Resolution Foundation.

Cox, George (2013), Overcoming Short-Termism, The Labour Party.

Cribb, Jonathan et al. (2017), Living Standards, Poverty and Inequality in the UK 2017, Institute for Fiscal Studies.

Crick, Bernard (1984), Socialist Values and Time, The Fabian Society.

Crosland, Anthony (1956), The Future of Socialism, Jonathan Cape.

Crosland, Anthony (1974), Socialism Now and Other Essays, Jonathan Cape.

Cruddas, Jon et al. (2016), Labour's Future: Why Labour Lost in 2015 and How it Can Win Again, One Nation Register .

D'Arcy, Conor (2017), Low Pay Britain 2017, Resolution Foundation.

Davis, Rowenna (2011), Tangled Up In Blue, Short Books Ltd.

Deming, W. Edwards (1982), Out of the Crisis, Cambridge University Press.

Felstead, Alan et al. (2007), Skills at Work 1986–2006, ESRC.

Felstead, Alan et al. (2013), Work Intensification in Britain, ESRC/ LLAKES.

Fevre, Ralph et al. (2012), Trouble at Work, Bloomsbury.

Ford, Martin (2015), The Rise of the Robots: Technology and the Threat of Mass Unemployment, Oneworld.

Foroohar, Rana (2016), Makers and Takers, Crown Business.

Frey, Carl Benedikt and Osborne, Michael (2013), The Future of Employment: How Susceptible Are Jobs To Computerisation?, Oxford Martin School.

Fukuyama, Francis (1992), The End of History and the Last Man, Free Press.

Gallie, Duncan (ed) (2007), Employment Regimes and the Quality of Work, Oxford University Press.

Gallie, Duncan and Zhou, Ying (2013), Work Organisation and Employee Involvement in Europe, European Foundation for the Improvement of Living and Working Conditions.

Gallie, Duncan et al. (2013), Fear at Work, ESRC/LLAKES.

Giddens, Anthony (1991), Modernity and Self Identity, Polity.

Goodhart, David (2017), The Road to Somewhere: The New Tribes Shaping British Politics, Penguin.

Gould, Philip (1999), The Unfinished Revolution, Abacus.

Grass, Gunter (1972), From the Diary of a Snail, Vintage edition 2000.

Green, Francis et al. (2013), Job-Related Well-Being in Britain, ESRC/LLAKES.

Hall, Peter and Soskice, David (eds) (2001), Varieties of Capitalism, Oxford University Press.

Hall, Mark and Purcell, John (2012), Consultation at Work – Regulation and Practice, Oxford University Press.

Harris, Seth and Krueger, Alan (2015), A Proposal for Modernizing Labour Laws for Twenty-First-Century Work: The Independent Worker, The Hamilton Project.

Harrop, Andrew (2017), Labour Must Return to First Principles on Child Poverty, Fabian Review, July 2017.

Hattersley, Roy (1987), Choose Freedom: The Future for Democratic Socialism, Michael Joseph.

Hendy, John and Ewing, Keith (2017), What Is Sectoral Collective Bargaining? Available at: http://www.ier.org.uk/blog/ier-fact-news-what-sectoral-collective-bargaining.

Hills, John (2015), Good Times, Bad Times: The Welfare Myth of Them and Us, Policy Press.

Honderich, Ted (2005), Conservatism, Pluto Press.

Hutton, Will (1995), The State We're In, Random House.

Hutton, Will (2015), How Good Can We Be? Ending the Mercenary Society and Building a Great Country, Little Brown.

Huws, Ursula et al. (2016), Crowd Working Survey: Size of the UK's Gig Economy Revealed for the First Time, University of Hertfordshire, UNI Europa, Federation for European Progressive Studies.

Institute of Fiscal Studies (2017), Manifesto Analysis Briefing, available at: https://election2017.ifs.org.uk/article/manifesto-analysis-briefing-23-may?_ga=2.140653680.353317573.1516953154-634724198.1516953154.

Inanc, Hande et al. (2013), Job Control in Britain, ESRC/LLAKES.

Jenkins, Clive, and Sherman, Barry (1979), The Collapse of Work, Eyre Methuen.

Jenkins, Clive and Sherman, Barry (1981), Leisure Shock, Eyre Methuen.

Kahn-Freund, Otto (1972), Labour and the Law, Stevens and Sons.

Katz, Larry and Krueger, Alan (2016), The Rise and Nature of Alternative Work Arrangements in the United States 1995–2015, NBER Working Paper No 22667.

Kay, John (2003), The Truth about Markets, Allen Lane.

Kay, John (2012), The Kay Review of UK Equity Markets and Long-Term Decision Making, Department for Business Industry and Skills .

Keynes, John Maynard (1931), Economic Possibilities for Our Grandchildren, in Essays in Persuasion, W.W. Norton Edition 1963.

Kitching, John (2016), Exploring the Freelance Workforce in 2015, IPSE/University of Kingston.

Kivimaki, Mika (2007), Effort Reward Imbalance, Procedural Injustice and Relational Injustice as Psychosocial Predictors of Health; Complementary or Redundant Models? Occupational and Environmental Medicine 64, pp. 659–665.

Kumhof, Michael and Rancière, Romain (2010), Leverage, Inequality and Crisis, IMF Working Paper 10/268, International Monetary Fund.

Lawson, Neal (2016), Social Democracy without Social Democrats, Compass.

Layard, Richard (2005), Happiness: Lessons from A New Science, The Penguin Press.

Le Grand, Julian (2003), Motivation, Agency and Public Policy, Oxford .

Le Grand, Julian (2008), The Other Invisible Hand, Princeton University Press.

Lindert, Peter (2004), Growing Public, Cambridge University Press.

Marcuse, Herbert (1964), One Dimensional Man, Routledge, 2002 edition.

Marmot, Michael (2004), Status Syndrome, Bloomsbury.

Marmot, Michael (2010), Fair Society Healthy Lives, The Marmot Review.

Marx, Karl (1845), The German Ideology, Progress Publishers Edition, 1964.

Mason, Paul (2015), Postcapitalism: A Guide to Our Future, Allen Lane.

McFadden, Pat (2017), A New Marshall Plan for the Working Class, Progress Magazine December 2017, Progress.

Mount, Ferdinand (2012), The New Few: Or A Very British Oligarchy, Simon and Schuster.

Nozick, Robert (1974), Anarchy, State and Utopia, Basic Books.

OECD (1994), The OECD Jobs Study: Facts, Analysis Strategy, Organisation for Economic Co-operation and Development.

OECD (2004), Employment Outlook 2004, Organisation for Economic Co-operation and Development.

OECD (2011), Why Inequality Keeps Rising, Organisation for Economic Co-operation and Development.

ONS (2016), Trends in Self Employment in the UK 2001–2016, Office for National Statistics.

ONS (2017), Overview of the UK Population July 2017, Office for National Statistics.

Orwell, George (1941), The Lion and The Unicorn: Socialism and the English Genius, Penguin edition 1982.

Orwell, George (1945), Notes on Nationalism, in Essays, Penguin Modern Classics edition, 2000.

Ostry, Jonathan et al. (2014), Redistribution, Inequality and Growth, IMF Staff Discussion Note, SDN/14/02, International Monetary Fund.

Painter, Anthony and Thoung, Chris (2015), Creative Citizen, Creative State: The Principled and Pragmatic Case for a Universal Basic Income, Royal Society of Arts.

Pensions Commission (2005), A New Pension Settlement for the Twenty-First Century: The Second Report of the Pensions Commission, The Stationery Office.

Pessoa, Joao Paulo and van Reenen, John (2012), Decoupling of Wage Growth and Productivity Growth: Myth and Reality, Resolution Foundation.

Pinker, Stephen (2018), Enlightenment Now: The Case for Reason, Science, Humanism and Progress, Allen Lane.

Plant, Raymond (1984), Equality, Markets and the State, The Fabian Society.

Rawls, John (1971), A Theory of Justice, Oxford University Press.

Rifkin, Jeremy (1995), The End of Work, Tarcher Putnam.

Roosevelt, Eleanor (1963), Tomorrow Is Now, Harper and Row.

Rose, Jonathan (2001), The Intellectual Life of the British Working Classes, Yale University Press.

Sainsbury, David (2013), Progressive Capitalism: How to Achieve Economic Growth, Liberty and Social Justice, Biteback Publishing.

Sandel, Michael (2012), What Money Can't Buy: The Moral Limits of Markets, Penguin.

Schumpeter, Joseph (1943), Capitalism, Socialism and Democracy, Unwin.

Sen, Amartya (1999), Development as Freedom, Oxford.

Sen, Amartya (2006), Identity and Violence: The Illusion of Destiny, Penguin-Allen Lane.

Sen Amartya (2009), The Idea of Justice, Allen Lane.

Sennett, Richard (1977), The Fall of Public Man, Penguin.

Sennett, Richard (1998), The Corrosion of Character, Norton.

Sennett, Richard (2018), Building and Dwelling: Ethics for the City, Allen Lane.

Smith, Adam (1759), The Theory of Moral Sentiments, Penguin edition 2010.

Smith, Adam (1775), The Wealth of Nations, Penguin edition 1999.

Susskind, Richard and Susskind, Daniel (2013), The Future of the Professions, Oxford.

Siedentop, Larry (2015), Inventing the Individual: The Origins of Western Liberalism, Penguin.

Srnicek, Nick and Williams, Alex (2015), Inventing the Future: Postcapitalism and a World without Work, Verso.

Sweeney, Ed (2015), Making Work Better: An Agenda for Government, The Smith Institute.

Tait, Cameron (2017), The Future of Private Sector Trade Unionism, The Fabian Society.

Tawney, Richard Henry (1931), Equality, George Allen and Unwin.

Timmins, Nicholas (1995), The Five Giants: A Biography of the Welfare State, Harper Collins.

HM Treasury (2003), EMU and Labour Market Flexibility, HM Treasury.

TUC (2003), A Perfect Union?, Trades Union Congress.

TUC (2017), The Impact of Increased Self-Employment and Insecure Work on the Public Finances, Trades Union Congress.

Van Wanrooy, Bridget et al. (2013), Employment Relations in the Shadow of Recession, Palgrave Macmillan

Wilkinson, Richard and Pickett, Kate (2009), The Spirit Level: Why Equality Is Better for Everyone, Penguin.

Woodruff, William (2008), The Road to Nab End, Eland Press.

Wright, Anthony (1986), Socialisms: Why Socialists Disagree and What They Disagree About, Oxford University Press.

www.ingramcontent.com/pod-product-compliance
Lightning Source LLC
Chambersburg PA
CBHW050524270326
41926CB00015B/3054